AF531344

Challenges in
Rural Development

Challenges in Rural Development

Edited by

H. K. Sinha

Executive Director

Lal Bahadur Shastri Institute of
Rural Management and Rural Development,
Patna, Bihar.

Discovery Publishing House

New Delhi-110002

ISBN: 978-81-7141-414-7

Challenges in Rural Development

Published by:
DISCOVERY PUBLISHING HOUSE PVT. LTD.
4383/4B, Ansari Road, Darya Ganj
New Delhi-110 002 (India)
Phone: +91-11-23279245, 43596064-65
Fax: +91-11-23253475
E-mail: discoverypublishinghouse@gmail.com
sales@discoverypublishinggroup.com
web: www.discoverypublishinggroup.com

Printed at:
Infinity Imaging Systems
Delhi

Preface

This volume embodies a number of papers presented at the seminar on **'Challenges in Rural Development'** organised by the Lal Bahadur Shastri Institute of Rural Management and Rural Development, Patna from the 28th to 30th October, 1994.

The idea of holding a seminar on this topic was conceived by Shri Ranchor Prasad, the then Chairman of the Institute. A large number of administrators, planners and social activists participated in the seminar and aired their views on the different issues involved in the theme. The seminar was inaugurated by the Governor of Bihar, Dr. A.R. Kidwai and concluded with the valedictory address being given by Justice S. Sarvar Ali, Lokayukta, Bihar. The broad areas covered at the different sessions of the seminar included the basic issues of poverty alleviation, the concept, models and approaches to rural development, its promise and performance, the strategies of rural development, hurdles and constraints retarding rural development, the linkages between various sectors of rural development, women's development and problems of rural health.

The discussions at the seminar were of a high order and towards the end an attempt was made to synthesize the findings and come to a broad consensus on making some recommendations for correcting the aberrations and speeding up the tempo of rural development.

It is our lasting regret that Shri Ranchor Prasad who also contributed an overview of the 'Challenges in Rural Development' could not live to see its publication, as he passed away early in February, 1996.

I am deeply grateful to Dr. H. K. Sinha, the Executive Director of the Institute for editing this volume. The views expressed in the various papers are those of the authors of the respective papers and do not represent the views of the Lal Bahadur Shastri Institute as such.

Sachchidananda
Vice-Chairman
Lal Bahadur Shastri Institute of
Rural Management and Rural Development, Patna.

Acknowledgments

It is great pleasure to present this book as a first publication of our Institute. The workshop on "Challenges in Rural Development" was organised on 28th October to 30th October 94, with kind cooperation of all the well wishers and patrons of this Institute.

Sri Anil Sinha, IAS, Secretary to Government of Bihar deserves our special thanks, for his kind efforts to help us organise this workshop.

UNICEF, Bihar, State Bank of India, National Bank of Rural Development, Sone Command Regional Development Agency, Bihar State Water and Sewerage Board, Bihar State Cooperative Bank Ltd., Bihar State Sugar Corporation, Bihar State Agriculture Marketing Board, Bihar Intermediate Education Council and Bihar School Examination Board deserve our thanks for their support and active cooperation in holding the workshop.

The Institute feels privileged and proud of having been benefited by the enthusiasm and participation of the renowned academicians, eminent educationists, distinguished journalists, researchers, workers and social activists, administrators, and industrialists, who at a very short notice had participated in this workshop.

The institute is grateful to National Institute of Rural Development, Hyderabad and Tata Steel Rural Development Society of Janandolan who had sent their representatives to participate in the workshop.

We are thankful to the staff, faculty and research workers of the A.N. Sinha Institute of Social Studies who helped in holding this workshop.

I am grateful to the Sulabh International Patna, in subsidizing the publication of this volume.

I am sure this maiden presentation of our Institute will be able to serve the people interested in Rural Development.

H.K. Sinha
Editor

Contents

I- CONCEPT

II POVERTY ALLEVIATION

III CONSTRAINTS IN RURAL DEVELOPMENT

INFRASTRUCTURE

List of Contributors

1.	Ranchor Prasad	Member of the I.A.S. held many important posts in Bihar Government and in the Central Government. Served as the first Chairman of the State Planning Board. He supernuated as Deputy Chairman of Bihar State Planning Board was the founder Chairman of Lal Bahadur Shastri Institute of Rural Management and Rural Development, Patna.
2.	S.K. Bose	Prof. Bose is an eminent teacher in Economics and was Principal B.N. College, Patna. Served as Pro-vice Chancellor of Bihar University and Chairman of Bihar School Examination Board.
3.	Sachchidananda	Prof. Sachchidananda, was Vice Chancellor of Ranchi University and was Director of A.N. Sinha Institute of Social Studies, Patna for about a decade. He is Vice Chairman of Lal Bahadur Shastri Institute of R.M. and R.D. Patna.
4.	Pradhan H. Prasad	Pradhan H. Prasad is an economist of national re pute. He was Director of A.N. Sinha Institute of Social Studies and is presently Professor emeritus there.
5.	K.K. Srivastava	Krishna Kumar Srivastave, I.A. S. (Retired). A former Chief Secretary, Bihar is associated with many social Organisations of this state.
6.	Shri Shankar Sharan	Sri Shankar Sharan, I.A.S. (Retired) was Development Commissioner, Patna. He is presently associated with many social activities in the State.
7.	S.K. Sinha	Shri S.K. Sinha is an expert of Cooperatives and banking finance. He was the Manager of Reserve Bank of India, Patna.

8.	Abhas Chatterjee	Sri Abhas Chatterjee, I.A.S. (Rtd.) is associated with social activities.
9.	Sunil Sharan	Prof. Sunil Sharan is an eminent Professor of Botany. He was the Vice Chancellor of Bhagalpur University.
10.	M. Mohiuddin	Prof. M. Mohiuddin is former Vice Chancellor of Patna University.
11.	M.K. Aggarwal	Shri Aggrawal is Chief General Manager, State Bank of India, Patna Circle.
12.	Kamlesh Kumar	Kamlesh Kumar was Head of the Department and Director of Extension Education, Haryana Agriculture University, Hissar.
13.	B.D. Prasad	Dr. B.D. Prasad F.R.C.S. is a famous Orthopaedic Surgeon of Bihar. He is a Social Scientist and Associated with many social activities of the State including PUCL.
14.	N. Prasad	Dr. Narendra Prasad FRCS is the most eminent surgeon of Bihar. He is associated with many social activities of the State.
15.	Hans Kumar Sahay	Prof. H.K. Sahay is Head of the Department of Economics, Patna University, Patna.
16.	Priya Darshi	He is a social activist and is working with Jan Sangarsh Vahinin Bihar.
17.	Gopinath T Menon	Shri Gopinath T Menon, is the Field representative of UNICEF, Patna.
18.	R.R. Prasad	Dr. R.R. Prasad is Director, Institute of Central Social Development, National Institute of Rural Development, Hyderabad.
19.	S.K. Singh	Dr. S.K. Singh is a faculty member of the National Institute of Rural Development, Hyderabad.

20.	Ravi Shankar Sinha	Shri Ravi Shankar Sinha was Director, Water and Land Management Institute (WALMI), Water Resources Development Department, Government of Bihar.
21.	Sachindra Narayan	Dr. S. Narayan is a faculty member of A.N. Sinha Institute of Social Studies.
22.	Raj Lakshmi Rath	Dr. Rath is a U.G.C. Scientist at A. N. Sinha Institute of Social Studies, Patna.
23.	Shukla Mahanty	Prof. Shukla Mahanty is Principal of Women's College, Chaibassa (Bihar).
24.	H. K. Sinha	Dr. H.K. Sinha IAS (Retd) is the Executive Director of Lal Bahadur Shastri Institute of Rural Management and Rural Development.

Challenges in Rural Development: An Overview

Ranchor Prasad

India still remains a predominantly rural country with 627 millions or 74.3 percent of its total population living in rural areas as per the 1991 census. Rural predominance is even more marked in the state of Bihar with 75 million persons or 86 percent of its total population enumerated in its far-flung villages in 1991. The percentage of rural population would be even higher if we take into consideration the fact that about 4 million persons, mostly agricultural labourers, were enumerated in other states or in urban areas in Bihar. The yearly, large-scale, out-migration of workers from rural areas in Bihar over the past three decades or more clearly indicates that adequate opportunities for gainful employment are not available as yet in Bihar villages, generally. The per capita income of Bihar is the lowest among all states in the country, and only about half the national average despite commendable performance by large profit-making industrial complexes such as Bokaro Steel, Tisco, Telco, and extensive coal-mining operations in the State. The Lakdawalla report (1992) shows that in 1987-88, the rural poverty ratio in Bihar was 52.6 percent and that during the period 1973-74 to 1987-88, it declined by 10.4 percent only as against 17.3 percent in India as a whole, and over 30 percent in Kerala. As the population of Bihar grew over the same period by around 30 percent, the number of persons below the poverty line in rural areas was actually much higher towards the end of the period that before. And, there is no indication of any very significant improvement in the situation in the years following. Although, it is fairly obvious that the painful situation that has persisted in rural Bihar, as also more or less in rural areas in many other states, agro-climatic regions and sub-regions in the country, can not be righted or resolved without giving concentrated attention and high priority to rural development. It has not featured prominently in the political and developmental agenda at either the national or the state level, it is only seldom that it features prominently even in media reports. There are also clear indications of the slowing down and malfunctioning of many of the programmes undertaken over the years by the Central and State governments for development for the rural economy and poverty alleviation. This is an urgent need, in this situation, not only for a careful, down-to earth review of the working of these programmes but also, more importantly, for some re-thinking on the entire issue for rural development. The Lal Bahdur Shastri Institute of Rural Management and Rural Development, Patna, decided accordingly to organise a 3-days workshop to consider both the conceptual and operational aspects of the rural development programme, with special reference to Bihar.

It gives us great pleasure to place on record the fact that this decision was widely welcomed, not only by learned bodies such as the National Institute of Rural development, Hyderabad, the Anugraha Narayan Sinha Institute of Social Studies, Patna, the Tata Research Institute, voluntary associations engaged in rural development work, learned academicians and retired civil servants, but also in an equal measure by important institutional agencies such as UNICE, NABARD, and the State Bank of India. The workshop was inaugurated by His Excellency Dr. A.R. Kidwai, the Governor of Bihar, who laid stress, among other things, on the need for development of literacy and education, high value crops, horticulture, besides rural crafts and cottage industries which would help members of the weaker sections such as weavers, potters, carpenters, blacksmiths to raise their income and living standards. He desired in particular that every effort should be made to ensure that the large funds provided by the Central Government for various rural development programmes are fully utilizes each year, with participation in such programmes by registered societies of beneficiaries, Panchayats, and voluntary bodies. The valedictory address was delivered by Justice Sarwar Ali, a retired judge of the Patna High Court and Lokayukta of Bihar who laid emphasis on need for giving urgent attention to all--round development of rural areas with special attention to problems of the weaker sections of the population, and expressed the hope that the main conclusions reached, and recommendations made in this workshop will be brought to the notice of all concerned, and pursued further. The papers presented at the workshop are being published in this volume as the views expressed and the data presented in them are likely to be of some value to both researchers and social activists engaged in rural development work.

A brief review has been presented of some of the more important issues raised in the course of discussion at the workshop in the paragraphs that follow.

There were differences among participants in the workshop in their approach to the problem of rural development, and emphasis on different facets of the rural development programme. While some participants laid emphasis on raising agricultural production and productivity on a sustained basis, development of literacy and public health, besides introduction of suitable measures for raising the incomes and living standards of people below the poverty line, others were disposed to view rural development as basically a strategy for raising in incomes and living conditions of people below the poverty line in rural areas. The latter view derives strong support from a World Bank publication entitled "*Assault on World Poverty, Problem of Rural Development*" which has been quoted at some length in Shri S.K. Sinha's paper on Problems of Rural Development. It is perhaps implicit in this formulation that development of the economy of the areas would be taken care of generally by market forces, but there was need for taking measures for alleviation of the poverty of the weaker sections of the population who may have to suffer hardships in the initial stages of the development of a free market economy. Over the past 25 years, the Central and State Governments have introduced a number of schemes which are all addressed to the issue of poverty alleviation in rural areas, mainly by helping people below the poverty line to acquire some productive assets of their own, such as a cow, a buffalo or a rickshaw with the help of Government subsidy and bank loan at a concession rate of Interest, and providing employment to agricultural labourers during the slack seasons. The Central and State Departments of Rural Development have thus been concerned over the past two and a half decades almost exclusively with the formulation and implementation of these programmes. In the Economic Survey presented by the Government of India to Parliament on the eve of the budget session, rural development finds mention only in one paragraph in the last chapter of the report entitled "*Social Sectors*".

The schemes listed under this head included Jawahar Rojgar Yojana, Employment Assurance Scheme, Integrated Rural Development Programme and Rural Water Supply and Sanitation. The total provision for these schemes during the years 1992-93 to 1994-95 adds upto Rs.16, 046 crores. There is also mention in the same chapter under the head "Welfare of weaker sections", of schemes for making available house-sites, and providing assistance for construction of residential units for the weaker sections of the population. Although some of the schemes introduced for alleviation of poverty, and bringing about some improvement in the living conditions of people belonging to the weaker sections of the population in rural areas were well conceived, and substantial expenditure has been incurred on these programmes, it can be hardly claimed that they have produced any very significant or enduring results, or set in motion a process of self generating growth of the rural economy and the rise in the incomes and living conditions of the people below the poverty line. There has been some reduction over the years in the percentage of people below the poverty line, but this is attributable to a variety of factors e.g. attainment of a high level of literacy as in Kerala, rise in agricultural production, and earnings of out-migrants, besides the impact of the poverty alleviation and employment schemes introduced by government.

There is no gainsaying the fact that, in the situation obtaining in rural areas in Bihar and India generally, high priority will have to be given in any plan or programme of rural development to measures for bringing about improvement in the socio-economic condition of the weaker sections of the population.

It has to be remembered, at the same time, that no enduring result can be achieved in promoting the development of any area, or of any section of the population living therein, without giving due attention to the development of the human resources and the production potential of the area, and build-up of the basic physical and social infrastructure required. After careful analysis of the issues involved, and the ground realities that exist in most parts of rural Bihar and rural areas in most other states of the country, we have reached the conclusion that enduring results can be brought about only if we take a comprehensive view of the situation obtaining in rural areas, and adopt, what may be called, a holistic approach to the problem of rural development. It has to be remembered that a rural development programme is essentially a plan of action for the development of an area or areas which are lagging behind in socio-economic development due generally to prevalence of very low levels of literacy and education, and heavy dependence on primary production viz, agriculture, animal husbandry, fishery etc., and where the distribution of productive assets, such as land, is highly skewed (giving rise to serious disparities in income levels), social status and development of social and physical infrastructure is lagging behind. We consider, therefore, that a plan or programme for development of rural areas in India generally, and more specially in the State of Bihar, should comprehend the following elements:

(i) Development of human resources including
  (a) Literacy, more especially female literacy, education, and skill development;
  (b) Sanitation and public health measures;
  (c) Family limitation;
(ii) Land Reforms
(iii) Development of the productive resources of the area;
(iv) Infrastructure development;
(v) Special measures for alleviation of poverty and bringing about significant improvement in the living conditions of the weaker sections of the population.

This was no doubt basically the idea behind introduction of an Integrated Rural Development Programme in the mid-seventies. Sporadic efforts were made initially to prepare integrated rural development plans for a few blocks and districts. This matter was, however, not pursued further, and although the nomenclature 'Integrated Rural Development' has been retained over the years' no serious endeavour has been made to integrate the programme for giving financial assistance to the people below the poverty line for acquiring some productive assets of their own, with the development plan of the block.

We may now review briefly the existing situation in Bihar in regarding to different facets to the rural development programmes outlined above:

(i) Literacy, Education and Skill Development. : The 1991 census figures show that Bihar has the lowest literacy rate, i.e., 38.48 percent, among all states in India. In rural areas the literacy rate for all persons, males and females together, works out to a meagre 27. 17 per cent; and for females only, to a bare 14.6 percent. For scheduled castes, the literacy rate was only a little over 10 percent and it fell to a bare 2.2 per cent for Musahars, a large segment of the scheduled caste population in Bihar. We may say, in other words, that about 73 per cent of the total rural population of Bihar, and over 84 per cent of the female population are illiterate. There is a close nexus between poverty and illiteracy, and it is mostly the people belonging to the weaker sections of the population who suffer most from this malady. There is clearly need for giving the most urgent atention to this problem for bringing about any very significant decline in the poverty ratio, and promoting rural development generally, in the foreseable future. We might mention here that there was a massive expansion of the network of primary and middle schools in the Bihar country-side during the first 10-12 Years after the advent of independence, and rapid spread of literacy among the weaker sections of the population during this period with provision of free studentship and stipends to students belonging to this category. There has been a slowing down of this trend over the past three decades or so due mainly to two factors: (1) accelerated population growth resulting in increase in the size of families and the number of young children, and the inability or reluctance of parents belonging to the poorer sections of the population to send their children to school, or to allow them to continue their study for more than six of 10-12 for the maintenance of the family: and (2) lack of proper instructional facilities in many schools, and inadequate supervision and poor management of primary and middle schools spread over the country-side. Parents of the children of poor families would be more inclined to send their young children to school, and to allow them to complete the primary education course, if primary school students are provided with mid-day meals in their schools at public expense. There should not be much difficulty in introducing this arrangement as we understand that the Government of India has now decided to give financial assistance to the states for this purpose. With the enactment of the 73rd Amendment to the Constitution of India and new Panchayat Raj Acts in the States, administrative control over primary and middle schools situated in different villages will now vest in the village Panchayat. The functioning of these schools would tend to improve if the Panchayats thus assume responsibility and control over the management of the schools in their jurisdiction, subject only to guidelines contained in the Education Code.

No serious endeavour has been made so far to impart vocational education to young students in rural areas. The TRYSEM scheme had condensable potential for giving practical training to young persons in different crafts and techniques for self-employment, but it has made only very limited impact here and there, largely because of lack of proper motivation and commitment to the scheme generally among the administrative personnel engaged in this programme and lack of awareness among the beneficiary groups about the scheme.

(ii) Land Reforms: that is, making structural changes in land-man relationship with a view to reduce skewed distribution of land, and generally improve the motivation of the tillers of the soil to raise agricultural production and productivity. Zamindaries were abolished in Bihar under an Act passed in 1950. Another law placing limitations on the ceiling of Raiyati holdings was enacted in 1956. Many large raiyati holdings have since been split and in size due to family partitions, land sales, gifts of land during the Bhoodan movement, and action taken by Government implemented effectively in many areas, and this has given rise to serious and continuing agrarian troubles and Naxalite campaigns, particularly in the lower plateau region, and the adjacent plains in south-central Bihar. The land made available during the Bhoodan movement and taken over under the ceiling law have also not been fully distributed as yet and there are also many cases where the land gifted earlier has been again taken possession of by the donor landdowner. The continuance of agrarian troubles in areas where the ceiling law has not been implemented satisfactorily is one of the various factors contributing to relatively low value product of agricultural production and productivity in Bihar. The large farm holdings that still remain are also not looked after satisfactorily and this also results in lower agricultural production and productivity, besides giving rise to social tension sand land movements. The wide-spread prevalence of the '*bataidari*' (share-cropping) system in the plains districts without any written contract defining the rights and obligations of the two parties is yet another factor contributing to low yield per hectare of land in Bihar. Bataidars do not have any interest to remain in occupation of the land longer than a crop season or so, and are not therefore, sufficiently motivated to make investments in land development and soil improvement and many of them also did not have enough means to invest in high-cost seeds and fertilizers which are needed for raising crop yields. The progressive increase, over the past decades or so, in the number of marginal holdings (below 1 hectare but above 0.5 hectare) and sub-marginal holdings (below 0.5 hectares) holdings is also a matter that calls for urgent attention. At the 1981 Agricultural Census, there were about 6.6 million sub-marginal holdings with their average size being 0.2 hectare only and a total area of 1.56 million hectares. Marginal holdings covered about 1.39 million hectares, with the average size or holdings being 0.7 hectare only. There is hardly hardly any doubt that since 1981, there has been a significant increase in the number of such holdings. As such tiny holdings can not provide livelihood to any average family of 5 or 6 persons and almost all young male members as the family have to seek employment in nearby areas or beyond, and even young children are put to work. It is thus seldom that these tiny holdings are on can be properly cultivated or looked after. The answer to this problem probably lies in constitution of cooperatives or registered societies of the owners of such holdings for proper management of the land, and distribution of proceeds. These are only very tentative suggestions. There is need for conducting field surveys for a proper assessment of the situation and formulation of suitable plan of action in consultation with the owners of such holdings.

The problem of land reforms is rather complex in Bihar, as the ground realities are not the same in all three sub-regions of the State viz. the north Bihar plains, the south Bihar plains and the south Bihar plateau. In the plateau sub-region, the main emphasis has justifiably been on restoration of tribal land to the tribals where such lands have been taken possession of by non-tribals in violation of legal provision preventing sale or alienation of tribal land.

In devising a proper strategy for bringing about effective land reforms in the plains sub-regions, due consideration has also to be given to the fact that the per capita geographical area and net sown area in this belt, are already very low. In 1991, the geographical area in the north and south Bihar plains was only 0.016 hectare and 0.020 hectare respectively, and the net sown area 0.011 hectare and 0.14 hectare respectively. While population grows, land does not grow. By 2000 AD, the population is expected to increase by 22 percent and the net sown areas will diminish accordingly. The netsown area will also tend to diminish with necessary diversion over the years, of cultivated land for infrastructural development, construction of more houses for accommodating the growing population and development of new settlements to relieve the existing heavy congestion and gross insanitation, especially in hamlets inhabited by scheduled caste families.

During the discussion or land reforms at the workshop, emphasis was laid mainly on ensuring effective implementation of the land to the tiller policy. Considering the crucial important of the land reforms issue for development of rural areas and reduction in the ratio and the complexities involved, there is need for more detailed consideration of the subject.

(iii) Development of the basic infrastructure required e.g. irrigation, roads, power supply. Fairly good progress has been made in Bihar in development of both flow irrigation and ground water development. It would appear, however, that only about 50 percent of the irrigation capacity created is currently being utilised due to heavy backlogs in command area development, inadequate and unstable power supply, and deficiencies in the management of the canal network, A large net work of roads connecting rural areas with market towns and the district and State headquarters already exists except for a few gaps here and there. The maintenance of rural roads has, however, been unsatisfactory, and needs urgent attention almost everywhere. Bihar has also an extensive net work of agricultural markets, but the manning of many of these markets has deteriorated a good deal during the past decade, mostly due to growth of administrative, complication and there is need for taking a fresh look at the organisational setup, and for introducing necessary reforms for revitalising the system.

For the development of the productive resources of the area we need to have a close look at both the agricultural and industrial sectors, Bihar is crippled by the low productivity of its agriculture. The key element in explaining the slow growth of productivity is inadequate and ineffective irrigation. Out of a total irrigation potential of 124 lack hectares only 28.4 percent has been created and even this is not fully utilized. Only 71 percent of the cultivated area is sown. 25 percent is left as follow and 3.4 percent is the cultivable waste. The fallow area percentage is roughly double that for the country as a whole.

The yield per hectare of rice is half of the national average and that of wheat is 25 percent of the national average. As a whole, the food grain yield per hectare is 24 percent short of the national average. The low productivity and slow growth rate in agriculture can be attributed to low adoption of HYV seeds, fertilizer, irrigation technology, in adequacy of infrastructure, institutional bottlenecks and natural calamities.

In the industrial sector after a decade or more of stagnation the state recorded an improvement in industrial growth. This was caused by the expansion of large scale industries both in the public and private sector. Besides, a number of large and medium industrial units were established. The state industrial policy has been announced. This will boost industrial development.

(iv) The two main infrastructures necessary for agricultural and industrial expansion are power and transport. Except in the coal fields and the industrial areas of chotanagpur, the development of power in Bihar has lagged behind other states. The mining and state plant loads have been taken up by the DVC and captive units, so that Bihar's own generation transmission investments are largely used for agricultural, commercial, Industrial and other domestic loads in north and central Bihar. The State Electricity Board relies, in part, on power purchased from DVC and NTPC. The per capita power consumption in the state is 125 units as against the national average 325 unit and 500-600 units in some other states. It is seen that the transmission grid has been expanding rapidly whereas the rate of increase in the distribution network has slowed down, The failure to complete projects according to plan schedule may be attributed to constraint of fund and to construction delays. The persisting power shortages in Bihar are largely due to low efficiency of operation of the system i.e. poor utilisation of the generation and transmission capacity that do exist. Some technical factors also contribute to low generating efficiency such as the poor quality of coal. To these may be added problems emanating from poor management skills, staff indiscipline, political intervention and frequent changes in top personnel. To remedy the state of affairs in this field, it is necessary to pursue a phased programme of inducting private enterprises in their field. This can be done by going in the for smaller power generation units. A network of mini hydel project may supply the needed electricity in parts of south Bihar. In suitable areas solar energy and bio-gas schemes can also be taken up.

Poor availability of power has led to low exploitation of ground water resources for irrigation and stood in the way for the adoption of high yielding variety technology. A large number of small scale industrial units have been seriously affected on account of non availability of power.

The other most important infrastructural drawback in Bihar is the poor development of transport. In 1987-88 only 35 per cent of the villages in Bihar were connected with all weather road. The length of surfaced and un sufraced road per one lakh of population is 35 km. respectively in Bihar, against the national average of 105 km. The rail road length has remained the same since 1971-72. Due to the lack of developed transport facility Bihar has been discouraged to grow commercial agricultural produce like vegetables, fruits, milk etc. In many parts of north Bihar not only is the cost of road construction high but there run across natural drainage lines. Apart from the trunk road a higher priority for link village road is called for. Attention may also be given to development of inland water transport.

(v) The primary aim of development is alleviation of poverty and bringing about significant improvement in the quality of life of weaker section of the population. This is extremely important in view of the fact that about 40 percent of population in the rural areas subsist below the poverty line. It may by assumed that there will be a decline in the proportion of poverty stricken population in rural areas as the productivity of major crops, wheat, rice, maize, pulses and oil seeds are increasing. Thereby raising the level of income of small and marginal farmers and also raising the wages of agricultural labour. Poverty reduction also calls for accelerating growth of dairy, horticulture, social forestry and fisheries.

The three kind of poverty alleviation programmes in operation are asset creation, self employment and rural works. All these need to be expanded in view of evidence of significant leakage under IRDP and ITDP, limited growth of entrepreneurship and the restrictive nature guaranteed manual work. If these programmes are operated under the guidance and control of new Gram panchayat, they can become more effective.

The extant of urban poverty in Bihar which is only an extension of rural poverty calls for direct intervention by the State to alleviate its effects. Slum, improvement has been stepped in the state through programme of providing houses to the poorer section of the population under the *Indira Awas Yojana*.

This brief introduction identifies the distinctive features of the rural development scenario in Bihar in mid-nineties. However, rural development cannot be treated in isolation. It is part of the overall-development of the state. Since the overwhelming population in the state resides in rural areas, our plea is that all development should be geared to rural development. Such a plea was forcefully voiced by the famous Tanzanian leader Julius Nyrere for theThird World countries several years back.

•

2

Development: Concept, Promise and Performance

Sachchidananda

Development is almost a synonym for modernization in developing countries. The first development decade was inspired by a some-what wholly charitableness of the developed countries towards the less enlightened countries in Africa and Asia, which had recently thrown of foreign yoke. The main objective was to achieve economic growth at a fast pace. It was only in the second development decade that there was reassessment of priorities and a deeper understanding of the needs of the third world countries. Just as the greatest hazard in capital intensive development is its potential to oppress the powerless by overwhelming them, so the greatest hazard in bringing in foreigners for development is its potential to undermine the powerless by deactivation them. This deactivating can occur when the foreigners take over, through excess of zeal or disrupts through incompetence the community's best developed energies. Experience of the development process revealed that the pattern pursued has depended upon dominances and exploitation and resulted in income inequalities. Although economic growth has been registered in terms of the per capita income and the gross national product; social and economic justice had been sidelined. By far the greater effort in development is and must be the effort of the powerless the and the hungry. In a study based on data from the developing countries, Adveman and Morris came to the conclusion that development has only made things worse for the poor. Hundreds and million of desperately poor throughout the world have been hurt rather than helped by economic development.

Development is not a gift from haves to the have notes. It is a right generated by conscientisation. The right has to be claimed and only then its fruits would endure. Achieving development may not always be a peaceful process. In a multi layered society that we have in India, resistence from the upper strata to the persistent striving of the poor is but natural. In such circumstances development may be a painful process. Development has to be self generated rather than imposed. Only then it can shake off dependency; local regional or national.

Julius Nyerare, one of the greatest third would leaders held that in developing countries all development should be geared to rural development. In India it is not so even when three fourths of the population lives in the village. India is conscious of its identity as a land of villages. Rural development as defined by the World Bank is simply a strategy designed to improve the economic and social life of a particular group of people the rural poor. Rural development has to be perceived as a process. It can also be measured as a product of a process. In our planning documents rural development is considered as the end product. Satisfaction of a set of minimum needs has been accepted as the cardinal indicator. The minimum needs include elementary education, rural health, rural water supply, rural electrification and housing assistance to rural landless. These items are mutually interrelated. In fact, integrated rural development is based on understanding the appropriate pattern of relationship of the different aspects in specific and historical context. It is also to be related to the over all national development, the patterns of relationship in various regions and the rural and urban areas with in the same region. When considered as a process, the approach to rural development has passed through several phases. In the first phase; it was believed that investment on a large scale would lead to creation of wealth to meet the needs of the nation. Once the products were there, distribution and utilization would follow. But soon it was discovered that even though wealth was generated, poverty was mounting. The malady was diagnosed as the invisible barrier created by traditional values and non rational orientation. This was sought to be corrected through winning over centers of community power structure and also by trans valuation of values through imparting new functions to the old symbols. But this also out to be a blind alley. Since early seventies growth with justice has been adopted as the proclaimed ethos of development. It is now accepted that justice has to be built in the process of development. Stress was also laid on people's participation for which a number of incentives and motivations have been provided.

(iii) India's commitment to rural development is long standing. The state policies and programmes atleast nominally reflect this awareness and demonstrate some concern for the rural sector. There is some ambivalence towards villages in the country's intelligentia. On the one hand, the rural way of life is idealised; the myth of the self sufficient and idyllic village community functioning in harmony on the basis of consensus. On the other hand there is acute awareness of the misery and poverty, ignorance and superstition which cry for a remedial action. This contradiction is sought to be resolved by planning for social intervention aimed at restoring the village community to its traditional pattern and prosperity. Gandhiji made his home in a rural area and initiated number of programme for village uplift. His 18 point programme was aimed to better their quality of life. Rural reconstruction was also dear to the heart of Tagore. After Gandhiji's death constructive progarmme were taken up by his followers through Sarvodaya and Bhoodan Movements. The aim was to build up Gram Swarajya in which the village would be the unit for all round development of the rural community.

In 1952 the Community Development Programme and National Extension Service were introduced in which the Block emerged as a unit of planning and development. The programme was aimed to be a cooperative endeavour with government and people as equal partners for all round development of the village. However, the assumptions on which the Programme was based were not correct. People were not enthused about the programme as they had no share in planning. Popular participation was minimal. The gain made under the programme went largely to the rural elite. The attitudinal change among the people did not occur. The high expectations aroused could not be realised.

In the early sixties the government decided to revamp the programme and concentrate effort primarily on increasing agricultural output through intensive agricultural district programme. Thus the state was set for the green revolution which occurred in some states in the country. Food production went up substantially and the country became self sufficient. However, it gave rise to new tensions and conflicts in the countryside. The rich became richer and the poor poorer.

In the early seventies the country rediscovered poverty. It was held that even after thirty Years of Independence 47% of the people were below the poverty line. The social services placed within the reach of the village people left much to be desired. In designing the strategy of rural development something positive had to be done to raise people's standard to living and to enrich their quality of life. The Janta Government which came to power in 1977 gave a rural slant to the entire planning process. More attention was paid to rural development particularly to the rural poor through the Antyodaya programme. The voluntary agencies engaged in rural development work were given due encouragement.

In the early eighties integrated rural development concept was introduced. It was aimed to make a dent in rural poverty. Assets were to be provided to the weakest section of the rural poor to raise them up from below poverty line. This was a target oriented approach to help the deprived and vulnerable sections of the population.

However, the functioning of even this programme has revealed a number of weaknesses. One of these is the large scale corruption involved in the whole process. A Prime Minister went on record to say that only 17% of the funds available for the IRDP reached the beneficiaries. The record of the past four decades of development has been largely one of non-performance. While the aspirations of the people has been raised, their hopes have been dashed to the ground resulting in large scale frustration.

(iv) It has come to be realised that the failure of rural development programme can be attributed in a large measure to working in a traditional society which is multi-layered and in which the social structure is not conducive to equality. The poor cannot lift themselves above the poverty line through their own individual effort. On the part of the poor, there are no compulsion of any kind to stay poor. They would certainly like to shed their poverty but the odds are heavily against them. The upper caste/class group is firmly entrenched in power. The poor are prevented by religion, by tradition and by other social forces to unite and challenge the position of the affluent groups. There is a persistent distrust of government officials and the poor are reluctant to participate in programmes designed for their development. The poor have very little access to information about various schemes. The way the development is designed and administered does not enthuse the poor. Every thing comes from the above. The top down kind of development planning excludes rather than invites participation of the poor in the development process. Tradition and development are not necessarily in conflict. Traditional social and cultural patterns can well be utilised to promote overall goals of development. Farmers may be encouraged to adopt modern agricultural practices so that they can use the additional income to meet family and kinship obligation. The authority of traditional leaders can be invoked in aid of development programme. Popular participation in development is facilitated where there is strong tradition of local organisation. It is also necessary that there should be complete transparency between the administration and the people. They should not be suspicious of each other intentions. Traditional values should not be used as an alibi for failure of government schemes.

(v) In this state of unrealised utopias and widening disparities, Panchayati Raj holds a great promise. The Balwant Rai Mehta Committee Report as far back as 1959 observed that unless representative democratic institutions were established at the local level and these were endowed with adequate powers and resources, local interest would not be a roused and local initiative in development would not emerge. The central as well as the state legislation on Panchayati Raj enacted in 1993 proposes to take democracy to the door steps of villagers. Through Panchayat Raj power and administration would be decentralised fulfilling Gandhiji's desire of Gram Swaraj. The Panchayati Raj institutions have been given constitutional status. The legislation also provides for the accountability of people's representatives. The Gram Panchayats have been empowered to supervise, guide and control social services. Reservations have been made for the weaker sections of the population.

They had been sidelined so long and their interests were trampled with impunity. In Bihar, Uttar Pradesh most of the Panchayats would have Mukhiyas from this group, as positions have been reserved for them. Participation of women have been ensured with the reservation of 33% of the elected posts of the Panchayati Raj for them. Full responsibility for rural development has been given to the Panchayats Resources for this would also to made available to them. The Panchayats would frame programmes for agriculture, industry, education, health and welfare. Panchayati Raj institutions at different levels would exercise effective control over their staff. It is expected that such control would lead to better delivery of services at the grassroot level. It is expected that with these steps people would have more opportunities for intense participation in social action for shaping their own destiny and social and economic justice would be available to the disadvantaged sections of the community. All this would lead to rural development at a faster pace and political power which had heitherto been confined to the national and state capitals would now flow to the villages and people would be able to shape their future according to their heart's desire.

•

3

Rural Development: The Two Models

Sachindra Narayan

Rural Development has emerged as a distinctive field of policy and practice and of research. This strategy came to be formulated as a result of the general disenchantment with previous approaches to development planning at national and sectoral levels, and it is defined by its concern with equity objectives of various kinds—specially the reduction of inequalities in income and employment and in access to public goods and services and the alleviation of poverty. It is this focus on distributional issues which has marked out 'Rural Development' as a distinct field, because an overwhelming majority of poor people in the developing countries live in rural areas. The World Bank, indeed recently defined Rural Development as a strategy designed to improve the economic and social life of a specific group of people—The rural poor.

The term Rural Development thus refers to a distinct appraoch to interventions by the state in the economics of underdeveloped countries. It is in fact a distinct appraoch to the development of the economy as a whole. It is more specific in the sense that it focuses particularly on poverty and inequality.

The expression of Rural Development may also be used, however, to refer to processes of change in rural societies, not all of which involve action by government. In this case the activity of Rural Development a form of state intervention must be considered simply as one of the forces concerned-although it is one which has become of increasing importance.

There was a report by Sri Bunker Roy in Delhi edition of the Statesman of May 9, 1996 on page 9 entitled Grassroot Struggle for a privilege. Mr. Bunker Roy maintains that "the crucial issue facing the rural poor today in India is very simple. Does a poor illiterate peasant, landless labourer, artisan and rural woman have a right to demand from the Government details of development expenditure a carried out in their village?

Do they have right to ask for copies of bills and vouchers and names of persons who have been paid wages contained in muster rolls on the construction of schools, dispensaries, small dams, and community centres that on paper have been shown to have been completed?

If they are willing to pay for these documents to be photocopied, which could also serve as certified copies in case any police cases have to be registered against village officials or politicians for embezzlement, corruption or misappropriation, can the Government refuse".

In 1990, a mass based organization called the Mazdoor Kisan Shakti Sangathan started working with the very poor peasants in an area that is openly acknowledged as one of the worst and most backward regions of Rajasthan--Bhim Tehsil on the borders of the three districts of pali, Ajmer and Rajsamand. The idea of MKSS was to find out the root problems behind the issue over non-payment of wages to workers on Government projects under the department of Forests and Public works.

At every stage they faced obstructions when they asked for information and details of expenditure on schools, dispensaries, drinking water schemes, rural housing dams and community centres. On paper they were shown to be complete but to the whole village it was obvious that some one had misappropriated the funds--school buildings with no roof, dispensaries with no walls, dams left incomplete and community centres with no doors or windows. The MKSS wanted the details everyone knew but no one wanted to say.

As in every Government, there are some bureaucrats who are concerned about funds reaching the poor and be spent wisely and properly. After years of knocking the doors, one young recently recruited IAS officer managed to extract some details from the Block office. In order to share this information with the public and with the people of same village (Kot Kirana in Pali district), the MKSS organised the first *Jan Sunwayi* (People's hearing) in the history of Rajasthan. At the outset, the MKSS had insisted it was a hearing and not a court (adalat). Every one was welcome to listen and respond--a politician, administrator, landless labourer and private contractor--and if they wished to say something to defend themselves the MKSS would give them the platform.

Corruption is nothing new. There is no one in the villages in Rajasthan who does not think that the village officials are scoundrels and thieves. So what is new? What can one Jan Sunway do? By reading the details of the bills and vouchers and names of people, they made it very personal. The audience who hear the names being read out how led and screamed at the brazenness of the officials and their elected leaders. In response was electrifying and all of a sudden it was no longer a game.

With the phenomenal response from the people to the first public hearing, several other public hearings were organized from December 1994 to April 1995 in the same region.

It was through this process that two demands emerged unanimously from all the public hearings. One, that any citizen from the village should have the right to make photocopies of all bills, vouchers and muster rolls on payment for any work done by the Government in their village. Two, that funds embezzled and misappropriated should be recovered from these village officials and politicians, their property be attached, and assets frozen and publicly auctioned and that the money recovered should be spent back in the same village. No departmental enquiry, no cases be registered—just return the money and let's get on with it.

In April 1995 in an historic announcement on the floor of the State Assembly, the then Chief Minister of Rajasthan declared that any citizen had the right to information. On payment, any one could demand and receive details of expenditure on work done over the past 15 years in their villages and all the documents could be photocopied as evidence should they want to use it infuture. Since India's independence, no State Govt. had ever made such a sweeping commitment and the coverage and vision of the Chief Minister was unanimously applauded.

With the commitment of the Chief Minister on the floor of the House, what had to follow were Govt. orders....

In a classic but anticipated instance of double speak, typical of Governments an order was hastily issued that very night. It made no mention of the right to photocopy documents but allowed for "inspection" and written details by hand with no certification possible...... What the Chief Minister committed on behalf of the Government, the bureaucracy manled and distorted out of sense and content.

In a sense, whatever the outcome, raising the issue of the right to information and demystifying it in a manner that every peasant, industrial worker and landless labourer now understands. The demand for information on development expenditure will increase.

II

The other case study is from Bihar of Manav Vikas Kendra (MVK) a voluntary organisation working among the Mushars of Jagdeeshpur block of Bhojpur district. Sri Mantosh Kr. Sinha popularly known as Mantosh Bhai, who left school on the call of J.P. (Sri Jai Prakash Narain) and joined the cadre of Chachtra Sangharsha Vahini at the tender age of 12. He was with J.P. until his death and he says that on the instructions of J.P. he started working among the Mushar of Jagdeeshpur. The area of action programme was also suggested by J.P. Jagdeeshpur, once upon a time in history has a glorious period because of being a place known for Babu Veer Kunwar Singh. It is in the Bhojpur district which is considered to be a disturbed district from law and order point of view. The Naxal activity was also there. These days the region is also known for socio-economic political tension. Though the place has remain a seat of political movement since historical days. Sociologically it has a mixed population. Mrs. Manju, wife of Mr. Mantosh is also an activist. It is an inter caste marriage arranged by J.P.

Mr. Mantosh and Ms. Manju went to the village and started living with one of the farmer. For six months they did not do anything except to mix with the villagers and teaching children of the village irrespective of caste. When they established good rapport with the villagers they gradually started meeting with the Mushars. After having complete detail of the Mushar of the each village of the block, they started identifying and contacting such voluntary organisation who can extend their programmes to these Mushars. Mr. Mantosh worked first of all to raise their economic standard, then to literate them and then to improve their health. In this endeavour after facing a lot of difficulty he achieved a little success.

But one thing in which he has succeeded tremendously is the Awareness programme. MVK has made each Mushar of his area of operation literate. MVK has made them aware of their rights and duties, MVK is now playing the role of a coordinator between Mushars and Block office. Therefore each programme meant for them now reaches to them without any extra effort. But even then some 'lapses' and 'gaps' remain their which draws our attention. I presume that the day on which such 'lapses' and 'gaps' will be 'removed' and 'filled' will be a red day in the history of Rural Development.

III

In recent days I have been reading news item, editorial and articles on corruption. It is being presented that a war against corruption has come up. But unfortunately it is not a fact. If we make a content analysis of the most of the published material we find that majority of these are for public relation work. How corruption can be removed when 48% population of the total population is still illiterate. Even after 50 years of the independence of the country we have not been able to provide majority of the population the minimum two meals a day. The drinking water, the minimum health condition and a roof over the head is a farcry.

Awareness of rights and duties of an individual is a precondition for the success of any programme. The provisions of the latest Panchayati Raj act if adopted may help in bringing change through rural development programme. These programmes again be made area specific and people specific. The target oriented programmes are the need of the hour. People must have right to information. Today we have isolated case of Rajasthan and a little similar case in Bihar but may be after ten years we will have more such cases. People should not be mistaken. When the people of India become aware they achieve Independence. Our history is full of such examples. From Chanakya to Gandhi we find the similar thing. Gandhi did nothing but except to make the people aware of the rights, duties and prevailing situation.

The two models of rural development presented in this paper suggest that the programmes of rural development needs a careful consideration at the thresh hold of 21st century. It needs to be considered as a tool of rural development rather than that of a tool of political development. The strong political will shown by the Chief Minister of Rajasathan probably will be of great help in developing the lot of the people residing in the rural areas.

•

4

Environmental Concerns in Rural Development

Sunil Sharan

Mahatma Gandhi had visualised Gram Swaraj through the conversion of the natural wealth of village into economic wealth having relevance to the day to day life. The pivotal feature of this economy was to achieve harmony with nature by creating a match between life styles and life sustaining capacity of the environment. Swaminathan (1991) points out that harmony arises from love and respect for diversity, both cultural and natural. Unfortunately, our emphasis on conserving diversity has been misplaced. While we have done nothing or very little to conserve biological diversity, most urgent in a biomass based economy like ours, we have definitely conserved the most undesirable form of diversity gross of inequity in economic and social conditions. Paradoxically, we keep harping upon our glorious achievement of being the sixth most industrialised country in the world, but we ignore the fact that India is also listed among the ten poorest country in the world with a per capita income which is 90 times lower than that of the highest income country, Switzerland.

Gandhiji used to say 'India lives in her villages' with a predominantly agriculture-based economy. What is the present scenario? The census figures tell us that with each passing decade, the proportion of urban population is going up (13.9 per cent in 1951 to 25.7 per cent in 1991). The craze for technology-driven affluence and consumerism is attributed to be the main factor in this tilt. The result is that the sustainable life-styles of the past are dwindling and, in the name of modernisation, highly inequitable systems of living are spreading.

Confining ourselves to the scope of the present deliberations, we would pick up the thread and first adopt the premise that conservation of biological diversity is urgent because loss of a gene, species or habitat reduces the available options. In our predominantly biomassbased economy, the livelihood security of the poor, both rural and urban, is seriously threatened by environmental degradation. In a meaningful programme for rural development, the fact has to be taken into account that with the change in the use of land, alterations occur in the nature of soils which invariably affect plant and animal life. Those who deal with evolutionary genetics and plant breeding feel deeply concerned about environmental degradation affecting soil erosion, gene erosion and rapidly dwindling biological diversity. We may now examine some of the environmental challenges affecting rural development, and the possible remedies through conservation of genetic resources.

Conservation of the Earth's Hardest Own Resource: Soil

According to Wes Jackson of Land Institute, Salina, Kansas (USA), agriculture as we know it, is destroying our top soil and polluting the atmosphere. According to him, this business of scratching the earth and sticking seeds in it is a recent notion, and on balance a bad one (Eisenberg, 1989). In the course of a century, a third of our farmland top soil, accumulated over millennia, is gone. Roughly, for every kilogram of maize seeds that a farmer grows, he loses two kilograms of topsoil. Soil erosion on a tilled farmland is mainly caused by rain; rain water takes away the runoff soil and loses it in rivers. In the river, the soil forms sediment and the nutrients in it cause water pollution. The Land Institute is dedicated to finding "low input, sustainable alternatives in agriculture, energy, waste management, and shelter." In his scheme, Jackson advocates ploughing of field may be once in five years and growing a mixture, or polyculture, of three or four crops nourishing to human beings or livestock. The yield of seeds per acre is like many existing crops. Special stress has been laid upon use of perennials with their roots undisturbed for years at a stretch. The roots would hold the soil in place, and would become adept at finding moisture and sustenance.

Undoubtedly, Wes Jackson has come out with a very radical view on the present day agriculture. It is also true that all traditionally known crops cannot be included in this programme, but various combinations have been suggested e.g., a forage grass, a legume, sunflower and wheat. It is heartening to note that our agricultural scientists have started talking about low input, sustainable agriculture. Let us see this agricultural process ever gets included in rural development programme.

Conservation of Fodder Genetic Resources

Our existing grazing land and forest resources have deteriorate to an extent that they are incapable of meeting demands of forage and firewood. Recent surveys show that our country is losing 47.500 hectares of forest cover annually. The trend started when pastoral economy gradually developed into agricultural economy with livestock rearing as a major component. The grazing areas were brought under cultivation of food crops, as a result the grazing pressure on forest areas increased manifold. Close and continuous bovine grazing in and outside forests resulted in the degradation of forests. The nutritious and palatable grasses were replaced by less palatable and inferior ones. Slowly and gradually, these areas were invaded by unwanted bushes and weeds like *Lantana. Parthenim*, etc. But these badly depleted areas can be brought to potential level of production through scientific management based on ecological principles of plant succession, cutting, burning, etc. Further ecological management that can be applied involves manipulation of various inputs i.e., rotational closure to grazing, removal of unwanted vegetation, fertilization, enhancing herbage quality and quantity through introduction of better grasses and legumes. Scientists agree that desertification of modern times is not due to any climatic shift but is man made. Grazing pressure has been greatly responsible for desertification. The remedy lies in collection and conservation of forage species of grasses and legumes. There is a need for identification and intensification of cultivation of high yielding genotypes. The genotypes with multiple resistance for the prevalent pests and diseases must be conserved and used. Since the grazing lands of India are mainly the savannas comprinsing shrubs, and trees besides the grass, silvipastoral management would indeally serve the dual purpose of forage and food production. Our studies spanning over a period of three decades on grasses of forage value have yielded valuable results from the point of view of genetic conservation and can find useful application in developing grazing pastures in rural areas.

Conservation of Gene Centres of Crop Plants

The major food and fibre plants that feed and clothe the vast human population were developed from their wild progenitors by stone-Age men, and, in this regard we cannot realise the debt we owe to them. The primitive agriculture relied upon three methods for increasing genetic variability: (i) Plant introduction, (ii) crop-weed complexes, and (iii) agronomic practice (Harlan, 1966). A new dimension was added to the modern plant breeding when the Russian agrobotanist N.I. Vavilov, through his explorations, identified 12 centres of origin of cultivated plants. These centres are now called the centres of diversity or gene centres. The majority of these centres lie in the developing countries and the Indian subcontinent is an important one. The gene erosion resulting from the improvident techniques of monogenic breeding and replacement of land-races and local varieties by highly uniform crops on a world wide scale threatens these vital resources. Gene erosion is also threatened under the increasing impact of the technological culture requiring removal of plants on a large scale for various projects. India constitutes the gene centre of a large number of crop plants and any erosion in this would mean that we shall lose an irreplaceable asset which was handed down to us by nature through millions of years of evolutionary process. A recent example is provided by the decision to save the Silent Valley in Kerala from destruction which would have inevitably followed the proposed hydro-electric project in that region. The wild rice discovered in the Silent Valley carried genes for resistance to a number of pests and diseases. Genes from the wild rice were successfully incorporated into the cultivated ones resulting in the development of rice varieties resistant to a number of pests and diseses, and the value and importance of this type of contribution cannot be assessed in material terms. Similarly, in future also, useful genes may be unravelled in other wild species which when incorporated into the cultivated species through hybridization may yield crops of great economic value.

Cultivation of Subsidiary Crops

Breading of monogenic varieties of crop plants is another danger facing genetic conservation in which the local varieties which were developed by our ancestors through thousands of years of conscious and subconscious selection may become extinct. Many varieties have already disappeared. Through our studies and publications, we have been advocating a case for adopting and encouraging cultivation of subsidiary crops on which we can depend when the monsoons fail. In subsistence farming like ours, no one can afford a failure. When the family is living barely from harvest to harvest with very little surplus as reserve, a failure means famine and perhaps death. A dependable crop therefore, is much more to be desired than maximum yield. The little millets are ideal in this respect. We have carried out studies in the little millet, *Panicum sumatrense* (= 'kutki' or 'gondli') which is grown in Bihar in Santhal Pargana and Chotanagpur. It is grown by the tribals on second-class lands at the beginning of the rains, and even in such soils which yield little or nothing this millet can thrive and mature a crop. Other millets like 'china' millet 'sama'.millet, and finger millet (='marua') could be considered as dependable crops on poor lands. Therefore, in any land use and agro-planning, it is imperative that we set aside some area for maintaining cultures of mixed populations, conservation of local varieties and development of dependable crops.

Role of NGOs in Rural Development

Nothwithstanding a certain degree of sceptism prevailing about the role of NGOs in rural development, there are may success stories coming out from different parts of the country and these organisations deserve support and encouragement. One such experiment comes from the Puri district of Orissa where residents of 1,200 villages got together to form the Brukshya

O Jeevra Bandhu Parishad (BOJBP) to protect their environment and devised quaint methods to regenerate the area ecologically. Seedlings are demanded as part of dowry and planting trees, instead of feeding Brahmins, has become a part of death ceremonies. Earlier the area was ecologically so degraded that even roots were being dug up, but today, the villagers cannot imagine cutting down trees. With regenerated vegetation, wildlife has also returned to forests which now have bears, rabbits, monkeys, pythons an d storks and other birds (Behera, 1992).

In rural development, the NGOs can play a very significant role if they adopt the working model on which the Shanti Sena is being trained at Gandhigram Rural University. It is a unique programme of training in non-violence and peace. Women students often take the leadership of Shanti Sena. They participate in Shramdan and Yoga and carry out three kinds of activities: C_1, C_2, C_3. C_1 refers to constructive activities such as tree planting, road building, sanitation drive etc. C_2 refers to conciliatory activities such as setting village disputes and resolving conflicts. C_3, even more important and interesting for the youth, refers to combative activities such as fighting social evils like alcoholism, drugs, dowry, untouchability etc. (Aram, 1991).

M.S. Swaminathan, the renowned agroscientist and thinker has been pleading relentlessly for the development and dissemination of "Green technologies" which are environmentally and socially friendly and can help to promote ecologically sustainable development. He, however, laments about the present state of our agriculture and says 'Our agriculture is becoming a sick industry as is clear from the need to write off farm loans from time to time, but we are avoiding analysing and solving the basic causes of the sickness"

As a plant scientist, I have tried to focus the attention of the participants of this workshop on some of the environmental challenges facing rural development. It is for the rural economists, sociologists and other activists involved in this area to analyse and provide solutions for tacking other basic causes that call for rural development.

References

Aram, M. (1991). Gandhian Experiment in Indian Education. *University News* XXIXI (2). 3-4

Behara, Chitta (1992). Planting trees instead of feeding Brahmins. *Down to earth*. 1 (3). 41

Eisenberg, Evan, (1989) Back to Eden. *The Atlantic* monthly November, 1989. The Atlantic Monthly Company. 57-89

Harlas, J.R. (1966) Plant Introduction and Biosystematics. In K.J. Frey (Ed.) *Plant Breeding*. Lowa State University Press, Ames, Lowa, 55-83.

Swaminathan, M.S. (1991). Educating for Self-Reliance. *University News*. XXIX (2). 69-72.

5

Rural Development

M. Mohiudin

When we think of rural development, we sometimes have a feeling that our five year plans meted out step-motherly treatment to rural development. We tend to think that since 90 per cent of people of India lives in villages, 80 per cent of the plan resources should have been spent for rural development. This is not perhaps a very realistic appraisal of the situation. The rural sector was not neglected by our plans, but it is a sad fact that it did not receive the attention it deserved.

India is a vast country. It needs all types of industries heavy, medium small as well as cottage industries. It was the vision of that great architect of modern India which laid the foundation of heavy industries in this country. As a result we established mammoth steel plants, locomotive, wagon and coach factories, aircraft industry, oil refineries, fertilisers and chemicals industries, dams and generation of electric power, and so on. The second plan had clearly stated that pyramids of big industries would be established, round which clusters of small industries would naturally grow. The establishment of big industries along with a chain of national laboratories immediately put India on the industrial map of the world.

We had the industrial policy resolution of 1948 which reserved almost all big industries for the public sector. This is quite another matter that our public sector undertakings were not managed efficiently and we incurred heavy losses. This fact coupled with the international situation due to breakup of the erstwhile Soviet Union and the emergence of unipolar world, has changed our attitude towards public sector undertakings. Now the wind is blowing full blast against public sector undertakings and for liberalisation and privatisation. Let us compare the situation in 1994 with that in 1954, when Indian National Congress held its session at Avadhi and opted for socialist pattern of society. Later, the Janata Party Government amended that preamble to the Constitution to constitute India into a socialist (and secular) republic. We keep an open mind on the issue of private sector and public sector, we are interested in the result. We are a little apprehensive of the foreign companies because of our bitter experience in the past with the East India Company. We do not want that multinational companies should introduce neo-colonialism in the country.

There was a marked difference between Gandhi and Nehru on approach to planning and development. Gandhiji was in favour of cottage industries. Even before India achieved independence, Nehru was chairman of the Planning Committee of the Indian National Congress. He was impressed with Western Industrial Society. He was also a fabian socialist. Gandhiji died in 1948, and Nehruvian model of planning and development was adopted by India. Despite its foibles and infirmities, the contribution of big industries to the development of modern India cannot be called in question.

Rural development does not mean development of agriculture alone. We must have an integrated approach and plan for the total uplift of our rural masses. Schomacher's concept of "Small is beautiful" or appropriate technology is admirably suitable for Indian villages. This is in consonance with Gandhiji's concept of vibrant, self-reliant economy for our villages. For this purpose we have to organise small and cottage industries on a large scale for our villages.

A word of caution is perhaps necessary here. We do not say that there should be two standards of living one for the rural masses and the other for urban people. The basic necessities of life like food, housing, clothing, health, education, some entertainment, some social services, some means of transport and above all work and gainful employment are essential for all, and we must try to achieve this goal at the earliest. The focal point of all development activities in the villages has been the Block Development office right from the first plan. All rural schemes of development are executed through the BDO. There was some legislations on land reforms; but land needs more fundamental reforms--regarding its ownership, clustering into viable farms and management by agricultural cooperative societies--without alienating the petty peasants and without allowing the managers of farms to grab all powers. Similarly, there is legislation on Panchayati Raj, but this has not been allowed to function properly. The Panchayts must be entrusted with responsibilities i e, (i) building of rural roads (ii) provision of drinking water (iii) sanitation (iv) control of buildings (v) primary schools, literacy and adult education (vi) primary health centres (vii) minor irrigation (viii) plantation of trees and other ecological measures (ix) cottage industries (x) co-operative societies, (xi) Lok adalats, and so on.

In fact, India needs a 4-tier government. Besides the national and state governments, there should be administration through Zila

Parishads and Panchayti Raj system. The National Government may take charge only of Defence, External Affairs, Currency, Railways, Civil Aviation, Communications etc. Other functions may be distributed to state governments, Zila Parishads and Panchayats. The last two may be given adequate powers and functions to act properly and effectively. There should be no provision for supersession of State Government, Zila Parishad or Panchayati Raj. The administration can be changed only by the will of the people.

Agriculture, being the main stay of our rural life, requires our utmost attention. Agriculture must be modernised by use of scientific tools and instruments, improved seeds, manuers and fertilisers, irrigation facilities control of pests and insects, and above all consolidation of holdings.

In order to facilitate the above measures, it is necessary to take some economic and social measures also, like provision of credit facilities at cheap rates of interest, crop insurance, warehouses, marketing etc. Similarly the farmers must be made literate enough to make use of modern scientific knowledge and research in agriculture and horitic culture. It was Gunner Myrdal of Sweden who in his book, *Asian Drama*, drew our attention to development of human resources for economic development. In 1988, the World Bank had made studies and found that investment at primary levels of education pays for more dividends than that at other levels.

A doubt sometimes lurks in our mind whether it is at all possible to solve the problems of rural India with limited land and almost unlimited population. The population is so large, so fast growing, so illiterate that what we gain by one hand is lost by another. Even if we organise agriculture on scientific lines and organise cottage industries on an extensive scale, still a very large surplus population will be left without any work. The only solution is to reduce our population. We must educate our masses about family planning first and then compel them, if necessary, to reduce population by incentives and disincentives. We must be prepared to take even unpopular measures and the politicians should be ready to lose elections. The task is so important that no other consideration should weigh with us. The surplus population must be reduced as far as possible, and we should try to give alternative employment to those remaining.

In England, there are big farmers and they are run by a few families. They use all scientific methods of agriculture tractors, sowers, harrowers, thrashers etc. The farmers union is very strong and agricultural prices are fixed after negotiating with them. The standard of living in a farmer's house is hardly different from that of their counterparts in the town.

There is an invasion of politics in rural India.

Politics by itself is not bad; we need it for the promotion of our common interest. But what is bad is partisan politics. All hopes of impartiality and justice are shattered when partisan politics rules a society or community, and it verily becomes a game of scoundrals. We must devise a democratic system for rural India where partisan politics is effectively curbed and controlled. We should try to restore the pristive simplicity and serenity of village life. Let me conclude by quoting from Gray's Elegy:

"Let not Ambition mock their useful toil,
Their homely joys and destiny obscure,
Nor Grandeur hear with a disdainful smile
The short and simple annals of the poor".

We propose a minor amendment to the above ideas. We no longer want the destiny of peasants to remain obscure. We want to brighten it. JAI KISSAN.

•

6

Rural Development Through Women programme

Sachindra Narayan

Development vis-a-vis women introduces new dimension to question of economic development and all related aspects. It does not merely mean the role of participation of women in economic development. Nor does it mean just the benefits women get from development as a specific and independent factor, development itself needs redefinition. A meaningful measurement also will not be possible merely in terms of the growth in income, savings and investment and capital formation or even agricultural and industrial growth. The human being has to be taken into account more seriously and development will have to be seen as a social process which offers continuous expansion of opportunities and the enhancement of human capacities as well as facilities needed to exploit them. Such a development will take place only when the triple evils of poverty, unemployment and inequality are simultaneously attacked and that too in such a way that all men and women can participate and also gain in the process.

Many issues hitherto not considered as essential ingredients of development would then become indispensable elements. There is need for fresh understanding of concepts like well being, equality, opportunity and awareness. The common belief that welfare of the household means equal benefit to men and women also has to come up for serious examination. The need to make institutional changes to promote better understanding and harmony between man and woman as well as recordering and recognition of the contribution between the individual and the society would also become clearer and urgent. So also the need to formulate and analyses programmes and policies taking into consideration the changes in the social structure and social norms, many more issues will unfold in the process of intensive studies and research.

From the time immemorial, women have enjoyed a high status in society and played a significant part in cultural, social, religious and political activities. Their participation in the economic activity is, however linked mainly with the industrial growth in different countries and it has now become almost a common feature in all the countries. The degree of participation varies according to the stage of development of the economy as well as the social-economic and political conditions and the social attitudes prevailing in a country. Further, their activity in economic spheres now not only covers the realm of industry, but has spread to other spheres which hitherto had almost been the exclusive domain of men.

In India, the entry of women in the economic sphere is, however, not a new phenomenon. It dates back to the functioning of the village community in which women played a distinctive roles in earning a livelihood for their families by actively associating themselves in the production and marketing of agricultural products and handicrafts. With the beginning of industrial development in the country and building up economic pressures on the village communities, due to various reasons, women also started migrating to the cities to take up employment in industry. Initially they were employed mostly on unskilled jobs and in many cases were paid wages even lower than the men.

With the advent of independence, a number of measures were taken by the national Government in granting women equal rights in matters of job opportunities, equal pay for equal work and in protecting them from exploitation and safeguarding their other interests. The preamble to the Constitution of India resolved to secure to all its citizens, justice, social, economic and political liberty of thought, expression, belief, faith and worship, equality of status and opportunity and to promote among them all fraternity assuring the dignity of the individual and the unity of the Nation. This means that Indian working women are entitled to equality in matters of employment opportunities with their male counterparts, Article 39 and 42 of the Directive Principles of state policy stipulate, protection to women workers from exploitation and secure just and humane conditions of work and article 46, which directs the state to promote with special care the educational and economic interests of the weaker section of the people is also regarded to aim at improving the employment opportunities and conditions, inter alia, of the working women. Further article 15 (3) empowers the state to make financial provision for women and children and article 16 (i) and (ii) guarantee equality.

Of late, it has been felt that the various measures taken by the Government for the welfare of women have rather adversely affected their employment, specially in traditional industrial and are thus proving detrimental to Statutory obligation, such as, payment of maternity benefit maintenancy of creches etc. In this context the National Commission of Labour had observed "this decline in women's employment has been more marked in the textiles and basic metal industries. The decline of women employment is attributed mainly to technological changes rendering the jobs held by several women workers redundant".

Rural Development An Incentive to Growth

Shukla Mahanty

India lives in the villages. This adage which emphasises the agrarian character of the Indian Economy and to which such pointed attention was drawn by Mahatma Gandhi, continues to be true to this day inspite of the industrial development that has taken place in the last four decades since independence.

For 'Rural Development', the improvement of agriculture is the most important requisite. Economic development implies an increasing diversion of labour from agriculture to non-agricultural sectors, i,e, industry and tertiary sectors. Therefore, agriculture must not on provide a surplus of food for the urban population but it must also to able to produce an increased amount of food with a relatively small labour force. One of the ways of doing so is by substituting animal power for human power or by gradually introducing labour saving machinery. If a country is seeking rural development, the economy should give priority to agriculture and its modernization with new technological inputs. The Government of India has given due importance to agricultural income with redistributive justice in the rural economy is imperative. It will lead to improvement in the economic conditions of the rural masses and raise their standard of living. This is in the interest of the industry as well. The increased purchasing power of the rural masses will provide a larger market for products of the manufacturing sector. Besides, improvement in agricultural income will lead to growing mechanization of agriculture and will raise the demand for industrial goods.

Prior to the initiation of planned development in India, agriculture was almost stagnant and the impact of scientific, agriculture was minimal. Therefore one of the important, if not the most important, tasks of planning was to develop a viable and productive agriculture to achieve the objective of self-sufficiency in food and requirements of other agricultural commodities besides increasing farm incomes. It is due to this vigorous and concerted effort by agricultural scientists, extension workers, policy makers, administrators and farmers coupled with large scale investments in the public sector that the country has reached new heights in agricultural production.

Total foodgrains production which was only about 50 million tones in 1950-51 reached a level as high as 151.5 million tones in 1983-84, an increase of more than three times. The production of foodgrains during 1992-93 was a record level of 180 million tones. The increases in agricultural production have mainly been achieved by increasing productivity per unit of the area of different crops. The farmers responded to price change and profit opportunities whenever they could and allocated in acreage accordingly. Whenever irrigation was introduced or existing irrigation facilities were extended further, the farmers took to the cultivation of more profitable crops which, in the case of foodgrains, turned out to be wheat followed by rice, giving up in the process the cultivation of coarse grains and pulses which increasingly became less profitable to grow.

Agricultural income is a function of not only the physical productivity but is also influenced by the price of products and inputs. Agricultural income can also be increased by undertaking development efforts aimed at increasing agricultural production and by giving price and marketing support and supplying input materials at reasonable prices. Although oilseeds production has increased significantly during the Sixth plan period, demand for this group of crops being highly elastic to changes in income, its growth has not kept pace with the increase in demand resulting from increase in both population and per capita income.

In spite of the tremendous development in our agriculture sector, there is still scope for development, particularly in the area of cultivation and in the productivity. It is not only in the context of fiscal in crease and increase of agriculture production that change is necessary, but what is more important is an increase in the agricultural income at the farmer level. In view of this we need to adopt an approach which will take care of both the structural and technological aspect of agriculture. The structural aspect becomes very important in our country which has a large number of small and marginal farmers who are not organized and who have very small farm holdings. Another aspect is the diversification of cropping patterns for motivating the farmer to give more attention to income producing crops. Market is another area which has to be improved so as to ensure a better price to the farmers. Timely provision of agricultural inputs supported by an efficient marketing system can definitely bring about an improvement in agricultural income. The links between the farmer and the industry need to be strengthened. The commerce and industrial sector should recognize the importance of agriculture. Their aims should not be profit-oriented alone but farmer oriented also.

If the doctors do not come to the rural area, if there are no banking facilities, then there will be no insurance facilities and it will become impossible to give loan and other benefits to the people. How much is actually reaching the real construction labourers or real landless labourers from various schemes (Food and Hunger, Food for work, etc.) is a moot point.

According to various sources, not more than 50 to 60 per cent of the benefits are reaching the intended strata. Besides, it is very difficult to get these schemes implemented in spite of all the resources at the district level and at the block level, and the good intentions of the Government nothing appreciable is happening in the rural areas and the income of the people is not rising. At the state level, this kind of operation is dominated by bureaucratization, and in the village it is dominated either by caste or by the sarpanch or by the Government nominee or by an M.L.A. There are leaders at the national or regional level who have no comprehension of what rural life is really like. Consequently, benefits are not reaching poor people.

Our economists, academicians industrialists and Government officials have always regarded agriculture as something which has to provide food and to produce raw materials for the industry. It has to generate surplus capital for improvement in the industrial sector because economic development for them means industrialization and nothing else. After 1980, one of the factors which retarded the industrial development was a lack of industrial demand and now it has been recognized that unless we give prime importance to agriculture, the growth of the economy is at stake.

8

Essential and Accelerators of Rural Development in Bihar A Broad Reflection

Kamlesh Kumar

Almost the whole of rural population in Bihar is dependent on agriculture: as owner cultivator, tenant cultivator, agricultural labourer, livestock keeper or village artisans rendering various kinds of services to the farmers. A few families small traders, for example, which may have nothing to do with farming are among the first to be affected by failure of crops in their area. The purchasing power of the people gets drastically reduced in case of crop failures. Thus agricultural development is imperative for rural development. It deserves the first priority. Only after agriculture gets moving fast that non-agricultural sectors of development will come into focus and will become meaningful. Attention to non-agricultural sectors of rural development will then become absolutely necessary not only to diversity the economic activities but also to provide greater inputs to agriculture. From then onwards the agricultural and non-agricultural sectors of rural development will be mutually sustaining.

The first and foremost thing needed for agricultural development is the 'market' of the farm produce. Conditions have to be created so that producer gets remunerative price of the produce even when he sells immediately after harvest and in his own village or nearby. For this, there have to be large number of vibrant regulated markets up to the Block levels. Before the ushering in of green revolution Punjab and Haryana had well managed regulated markets besides consolidated land holdings. Without these and inspite of excellent irrigation systems the impact of green revolution would have been weak.

It is necessary, but not enough, to announce procurement price of crops before sowing. What is also needed is to have adequate number of procurement centres distributed all over the state. If number of procurement centres in Haryana gets reduced by 20 per cent and these be started a week later than it is normally started and wound up a week earlier, the price of wheat will crash. As a consequence, the production of wheat in the following year will go down.

Profit is the strongest motive for producing more. Increased profit also makes it possible to invest more in inputs to increase production. The history of agricultural development throughout India or the world is full of cases of production going down in absence of 'market' for the product.

"Constantly changing agricultural technology' is also an essential need for agricultural development. It is now appreciated by all that farm science and technology is changing very fast and there is need for continuous research in all relevant fields of agricultural sciences to generated ever improving agricultural production technology. Agricultural technology is so much region and climate specific that scope for imparting agricultural technology by Bihar from other states/countries is very limited. Even the imported technology will require local adaptive trials. Bihar has to have its own well staffed and well financed agricultural research systems. Bihar is exceptionally fortunate to have its own pool of agricultural scientists comparable to the best in the country. Punjab and Haryana did not have this advantage when they started their agricultural universities in 1962 and 1970 respectively. They drew well trained agricultural scientists from all over the country. Bihar has been among the major contributing states. Only thing that has been keeping agricultural research, practically, in a state of suspension, in Bihar is the lack of funds. One can argue that poor Bihar is not able to finance research. Even the best of problem-oriented agricultural research should not cost more than twenty five to thirty crores in a year. This is not at all a big amount considering its importance in Bihar economy. Bihar must be already spending a few crores on them. This is only on the pay of the scientists. They are idle for want of contingencies and equipments. The whole of agricultural research set-up is and it should be with the two agricultural universities in Bihar, namely, the Rajendra Agricultural University, PUSA and the Birsa Agricultural University, Ranchi. Both of these universities are in pitiable condition for want of fund. The universities are not even able to pay regularly monthly salary to the staff. Bihar government should consider financing the agricultural universities as committed expenditure. Another thing to boost agricultural research will be to have good leadership in the universities. The agricultural universities in Bihar during the last 25 years had only a period of five years or so under dynamic Vice- Chancellors. This also requires to be ensured.

Agricultural production takes place not in a very big factory. Its lakhs of factories (farms) are scattered over the whole state and are owned and managed by lakhs of owners (farmers). Agricultural produce are pooled to the central places by the traders, government and the farmers. Similarly agriculture inputs are to be transferred to all the farms. The transport both ways is of bulky materials which cannot be efficient or even satisfactory without modern transport system. For this a network of all-whether pucca roads is a must. That network of pucca roads is an essential for agricultural and rural development it has been appreciated from the beginning of agricultural development in India or in any other country. Agricultural Economists say that a community (village) has to pay for the roads whether has it or not. It pays more if it has not. The cost of medical treatment, schooling, transport of agricultural inputs and output etc. are many times higher in absence of pucca roads. That road is essential for agricultural development can also be illustrated by government's own actions even in the thirties and forties of the current century. When government became committed to increase sugarcane production, may be as a result of powerful lobbying by the sugarcane factories, then it constructed some pucca roads in some of the factory areas from agricultural fund for the transport of sugarcane to factories. I came across the cement concrete roads in the interior of Dehri-on-sone community development Block towards the end of fifties. But construction of pucca and that too a network of these in the rural areas will certainly require enormous amount of money. Normally this should not be possible in near future despite the best of intentions on the part of the government. However, I dare make a suggestion taking into account the broad rural development scenario in Bihar that good network of roads can be gradually developed in Bihar without providing heavy budget for the roads. The statement requires elaboration.

These days there is liberal central funding for rural development. Most of the schemes under Integrated Rural Development Programme are employment oriented which in turn calls for operation of large number of Hard Manual Labour (HML) schemes in one form or the other. If we can divert all these schemes towards the road construction, major part of the road expenses would be covered by the IRDP Funds. The kachha work and full labour cost can come from that. Government expenditure may just come down to one third or one-fourth of the total amount needed. Further that amount can also be very soon (in a year or two) mopped up from the concerned area by laying toll tax on important rural roads. Even sharamdan can be organised and local donations for roads can be mobilised.

Based on my working with people in Bihar I can say that people's cooperation in all forms comes spontaneously if they are convinced of the sincerity of the development agency—governmental or non-governmental. This may appear to be loud thinking or even fantastic. But I am sure about the success which largely comes from my own experiences of working for agricultural development in different parts of Bihar and from my continued observation of developing Bihar from far away Haryana. An executive officer of Gaya Municipality became dynamic and told the citizens that if they paid arrear municipal tax, the road in front of their houses will be repaired. The payment came on and roads were repaired or new concrete roads were built. In any case the idea deserves a sincere trial by sincere development workers. This idea of utilising rural employment schemes for developing roads and other infra-structure has been followed in Maharashtra right from middle of sixties, with greater success.

All say and believe that effective land reforms are also essential for agricultural development. Land reforms, in Bihar, has been in process from the beginning of independence but it continues to be incomplete even after half a century. Therefore mentioning this as an essential, though significant, is to a great extent a redundant idea. Therefore, I do not seek to suggest any thing on land reforms so far its distributive aspect is concerned— an important aspect which is generally taken as the totality of land reforms. I wish to emphasis on the consolidation of holdings which by itself might double the agricultureal production. It is only then that every farmer can create his own source of irrigation (well, tubewell, reservoir etc.) Bihar is very rich in underground water both qualitatively and quantitatively. Every village requires for the general good of village some common land which before zamindari abolition were of two categories "Gair Mazrua Khas" and "Gair Mazrua Aam". The zamindars disposed of most of the Gair Mazrua Khas land and the village community gradually swallowed all the Gair Mazrua Aam land by encroachment. Now common land have to be again created. This is possible only during the process of land consolidation.

Another aspect of land reforms which is very significant and deserves urgent attention is fixing the lower limits of landholding. Higher limits of land holding under different situations have been fixed but not the lower limits. Unless this is done, very soon the land holding size will become too small to be economically viable. This would hamper adoption of scientific production technology. Fixing lower limit might seem impossible but there seems to be no escape from that. It would not be wrong to say that Nation as a whole has shifted from the ideology of socialism to one of capitalism even though the use of world "Capitalism" may not be acceptable to us. Privatisation, liberalisation and globalisation of economy, mean capitalism. Thus each of the farms and farmers have been exposed to global competition. The situation is going to be that of "compete or perish". This situation is likely to prove very advantageous and suitable for some of the states like Maharashra, Punjab and Haryana which are producing for export.

Thus, the only solution seems to be of organising small cooperative societies at the village level. There may be more than one in a village affiliated to bigger societies at the Panchayat, Block and District and state levels. Let there be as many federal set-ups of cooperatives as needed. Individual farmers may not have the experitise and experience for global competition. But these cooperaties can face the challenge of global competitions.

As an accelerating force, agricultural extension system can show extraordinary results, once essentials mentioned above are provided. What has been so far done, in Bihar and some other states is that intensive net work of agricultural extension services have been provided which are not giving as good results as possible in absence of infrastructure (essential) for development. Bihar has excellent agricultural extension set-up but its workers are demoralised for want of supervision, guidance and encouragement. They are simply banged and condemned if targets are not achieved. Supervision, as different from administration, and in addition to administration is needed. However, it needs to be emphasised that even a well supervised and spirited agricultural extension agency cannot do much in absence of good technology and infrastructure. It may be like putting cart before horse. The Haryana State which came into being on the 1st of November, 1966 was deficit in food. By 1969-70 it became surplus and started contributing to the national food basket. How could this magic happen? The time coincided with introduction of high yielding varieties of paddy, wheat and bajra, each village was linked with pacca road and was electrified, irrigation was expanded. These together did the magic.

There is a very wrong and discouraging belief in Bihar and more than outside the state that people of Bihar are backward. I can say with full sense of responsibility that this is not at all correct, after having close interactions with rural people of Bihar for 15 years and Haryana people for 25 years. Bihar farmers are, at least, as progressive as Haryana and Punjab farmers. Again the whole concept of people being considered backward and progressive has undergone a change. This is believed to be now simply an excuse for not developing a region. The noted economist Prof. Galberts has said that describing some people as backward "is a very often mentioned unmentionable".

Another thing that is said about Bihar is that the law and order situation is hoplessly bad. One must admit that our position in this regard is really bad. But this type of condition is now prevailing in almost all the states. Only patterns of violence differ. This has been accepted as a continuing phenomenon. Again the condition is not so bad in Bihar as it is made out to be by people outside Bihar. Agricultural and rural development is not all being seriously hampered by the unsatisfactory law and order situation. Agricultural production of Punjab continued to increase even in the years of terrorism. But this could definitely increase at faster rate in absence of terrorism. Agricultural development process should not wait for the improvement in law and order situation. May be that law and order situation improves as a result of agricultural and rural development.

Importance of Interdisciplinary Training and Research in Irrigation Management

R.S. Sinha,

Synopsis

It is hoped that India's optimally utilisable potential will be developed by 2040 A.D. Beyond that, the only hope to keep the food production level of the nation compatible with the ever-increasing population lies in "Irrigation Management". The two weaknesses of Irrigation Development sector of the country are: progressively increasing gap between created and utilised potential and comparatively one of the lowest productivity level in the world. The solutions to these twin problems demand shifting the irrigation strategy from 'protective' to 'productive' which needs comprehensive interdisciplinary training and research activities in irritation management. Scope and importance of such training and research activities in different aspect of land and water management for appropriate decision making regarding strategy, technology transfer, economic viability, and participation of beneficiary farmers leading to long term sustainability of the irrigation systems.

Introduction

The ultimate objective of India's irrigation development is to increase agricultural production to make it compatible with the sustenance requirement of ever-increasing population. In this context, the national target is to achieve a growth rate of 6.00% as compared to historical growth rate of 2.8%. The reaping of maximum benefit from the already completed projects through efficient irrigation management is, therefore, a priority task as envisaged in the "National Water Policy" 1987.

The Irrigation Development Strategy adopted over 30 years since independence till sixth Five Year Plan (1985) has been rapid irrigation development where project achievement had been measured by mere potential created rather than efficiency in irrigation management. With this aim in view, starting from 22.6 mha. of created potential before Independence, the achievement till 1990 has been 78 mha. of created potential of irrigation and it is expected that by 2040 A.D. ultimate utilizable potential of 113.5 mha. will also be achieved. Though this strategy helped in achieving the objectives of famine prevention and extensive irrigation, little could be realised towards assured, reliable, equitable and adequate supply to farms. This resulted in wide progressive gap between the potential created and potential utilised (table 1).

As this strategy did not consider the importance of irrigation management and ignored the intricacies of soil-plant water and yield relationships, yield over the irrigated land remained one of the lowest in the world inspite of all the development in Irrigation sector (Table 2).

Table 1

Irrigation Potential Created and utilised in respect of Major and Medium Project in India.

Plan	Cum Ir. Potential in M.Ha.	Utilised M.HA.	Percentage Utilised	Lag Utilisation M.Ha.
IV Plan (69-74)	20.7	18.7	90.8	2.0
V Plan (75-80)	26.6	22.6	85.0	4.0
VI Plan (81-85)	30.5	25.0	83.3	5.5
VII Plan (85-90)	40.0	32.0	80.0	8.0

Table 1

Yield of Major Crops in India vis-a-vis other Countries of the World.

Countries	Yield in Tones per Ha				
	Rice	Wheat	Maize	Pulses	Sugarcane
India	1.87	1.39	1.13	0.49	53.62
China	3.55	--	2.96	--	--
Russia	4.02	1.45	3.27	1.46	--
U.S.A.	4.95	2.05	5.70	0.88	81.77
Maximum Possible Yield	(6-8)	(4-6)	(6-9)	(1.5-2)	(110-150)

The other aspect of the problem is regarding availability of water and land resources supporting one of the largest population of the world. Our country supports 15% of the world population on 2.5% of land and 4% of water resources and is, therefore, subjected to much more stress than the other countries. To cope with this situation the country needs change in the irrigation development strategy from protective to productive. The huge financial requirements for providing new irrigation systems, the progressive gap in created and utilised potentials and the lowest productivity in irrigated agriculture now call for modern and scientific concepts of water and land management in evolving new strategies for operating the existing irrigation system at higher efficiencies giving higher production and productivity. To accomplish this task, the nation needs a trained management force of both irrigation managers and beneficiaries which can be possible only through extensive training and research activities in the field of irrigation management.

2. Need for Interdisciplinary training and research for irrigation management:

The inherent problems of lower irrigation potential utilisation and productivity can be attributed mainly to the below mentioned reasons:

(a) Lack of well designed and constructed distribution network with adequate number of control and regulating structures including water courses, field channels and on-farm development.

(b) Lack of well thought processive operation and maintenance planning for the system based on realistic to available supply and demand situations of irrigation water.

(c) Lack of micro-distribution in most of the irrigation commands.

(d) Inadequate land management planning such as land consolidation, levelling, grading, soil testing etc.

(e) Unrealistic and unscientific estimations and assumptions regarding cropping patterns, irrigation intensities, conveyance and application losses, Crop-Water demand and periodic delivery rate requirements.

(f) Faulty irrigation application methods and inadequate drainage facilities.

(g) Lack of adequate agricultural and agronomic demonstration, training and extension facilities to farmers.

(h) Lack of adequate inputs and infrastructural facilities.

(i) Lack of farmers participation in management.

It is transparent from the above faults with our irrigation management that the design of irrigation system for long term stability must include not only engineering aspects of conveyance and delivery but also agricultural, agronomical, social, political, economical, legal and environmental considerations. An interdisciplinary approach, in which each specialist understands the interaction between his discipline and that of his co-workers, is required to integrate these various factors into final system design. This can be achieved only through vigorous interdisciplinary training and research activities in the field of irrigation management for adequate searching solutions to the problems of the system. The concept of diagnostic analysis and action research has to be made clear to the water managers, beneficiaries and other involved agencies of scientific, realistic and cost effective solutions to irrigation project implementation, operation and maintenance needs. Significant improvement can be possible in the performance of existing irrigation systems without going in for huge capital investment in remodelling or modernisation of the system if proper attention is paid to interdisciplinary training and research activities in land and water management. The knowledge and skills so gained can be very useful for optimal utilisation of the already created facilities. Some of the multi-disciplinary subjects involved with irrigation management where training and research activities only can provide answers to their viability for the system are discussed below.

2.1 Crop Yields and Evapotranspiration

Though crop yields are affected by variables such as plant nutrients, weed and insect controls, cultural practices, crop varieties, plant density etc., however, if the water is the 'limiting factor', its effect usually dominates crop yields and there is generally a linear relationship between the crop yields and crop evapotranspiration or irrigation deficit. At certain growth stages crop yields are more sensitive to evapotranspiration for irrigation deficit. At the other stage of growth, crop yields are less sensitive to evapotraspiration devidits. There is a need of training and also research on the aspect of crop yield and evapotranspiration relationships as by its proper understanding limited water availability can be utilised for higher overall production by judiciously allowing more stresses to evapotranspiration needs of crops at stages of growth when they are less sensitive to water deficit. Such practices in irrigation management will improve economy of the completed projects.

2.2 Farming Risk Reduction

Training and research on farming risk reduction activities such as adequate crop qualities, varieties, plant densities, micronutrient applications, pest control measures are must for productive irrigation along with optimal water application. These activities vary widely from one region or environment to the other. The disciplines which cover these subjects are different from irrigation engineering and water managers and beneficiary farmers both need to have some concrete idea about them.

2.3 Irrigation Uniformity, Application and Conveyance Efficiencies

The desirable irrigation system is one which applies water most uniformly over the field. The uniformity of water application is directly linked with the flexibility of the system. More uniform application needs highly flexible system and inherent higher cost involved in its installation. Hence the profit from extra yield at a given point is offset by extra cost of providing higher uniformity for the yield. Similar is the case achieving extra yields by improving application of conveyance efficiencies. Therefore the optimal and marginal management in which extensive research is desired for deciding the level of management.

Most surface systems do not provide as accurate or as uniform irrigation as that obtained with pressurised systems because surface systems are line sources which are space and time dependent. On the other hand moving sprinklers, spray, trickle or drip systems, pressurised tubewell irrigation system are point sources in which desired uniformity can be achieved at wish as they are not time and space dependent. However, they are much more expensive and power dependent than surface line systems. A decision has to be taken whether the extra cost of improved systems providing better water control can be offset by benefits such as higher yields/reduced water application costs. When the cost of water is low, it may be less expensive to apply more water than to increase the level of management by upgrading the system. Similarly if management inputs are low, increased yields and reduced costs can result from improvement of irrigation system. Therefore, there exists uncertainty in economy of irrigation management strategies which can be resolved only through deep research activities and detailed studies of alternatives by thoroughly trained personnel.

2.4 Operation Management Strategies

Before deciding the management strategies, one has to be familarised with the physical, agricultural, environmental, social, political and economic aspects of the irrigation system which is possible only through a team of interdisciplinary group of water managers who have understanding of related disciplines over and above exhaustive knowledge and skill of his own discipline, the strategy can be "land limited" if the available land can be irrigated and enough water is available in the system to meet the optimum water needs. The strategy may be "water limited" if all the available land is to be irrigated with available water due to prevailing socio-economic situation or constitutional obligations. Sometimes social need of growing a particular crop in the area may require the management strategy to be "crop limited". When the adopted strategy is "land limited" the training and research need will focus attention on maximisation of yield per unit of land by evolving efficient" on demand" water allocation and distribution system. On the other hand, if the adopted strategy is "water limited" training and research activities will strive to evolve allocation and distribution system related to rotation, WARABANDI, and equitable distribution etc.

2.5 Training and Research needs for Accurate Irrigation Scheduling

The efficiency of an irrigation system is judged by the accuracy of delivery as per irrigation depth requirements during each schedule depending growth stages and plant root depths. Allowable soil water depletion methods, allowable soil water tension and allowable plant water stress measurement methods are commonly utilised for irrigation scheduling of non pounded crops. Pond depletion observation on daily water balance basis is the scientific methods of scheduling for ponded crop like paddy. Computer aided methods has also been developed for irrigation scheduling. Soil stresses can be measured with the help of tensiometer, neutron probe, or electrical resistance blocks. Plant based stress measurement is done with the help of infrared thermometers. Extensive training is needed for water managers and farmers both to adopt these scientific concept of irrigation scheduling. Also irrigation scheduling for each system will have to be evolved through extensive research as it will be unique in nature and will be influenced by physical, economical, agricultural, environmental and social parameters of area or operation.

3.0 Training to Farmer's for Participative Management

In India, the participative management of farmers is lacking. As a result, the irrigation system maintenance and operation is becoming problematic day by day. Whereas in developed countries, the farmers manage the entire irrigation system through their own organisational setup. In India irrigation water user's associations are few and far between even at minor or water courses level. Now it is accepted fact that efficient irrigation management is possible only through the participative involvement of farmers. Hence, farmers need to be given appropriate, training in participative management, socio - economic aspects, agriculture extension for their motivation and involvement in irrigation management.

4.0 Research Needs for Developing New Technologies for Irrigation Management.

New technologies are emerging and being adopted in developed part of the world in the field of land and water management. There is need for continuous research for evolving and adopting these new technologies in irrigation management of this country. Once the new technologies are adopted, extensive training is must to the irrigation managers. Emerging new technologies can be grouped in several categories like physical components, management components such as automatic scheduling and biological components such as plant modifications.

4.1 Physical Components

Innovations like surgeflow system, low energy precision applicators, central pivot computer controlled sprinkler system, lateral movement automatic sprinkler system, drip, trickle and double irrigation system, laser controlled land levelling, automatic canal operation control systems, multifunctional irrigation systems are some of the new frontiers of modern physical components of irrigation system. A day is not far-off when India will have to adopt these modern physical components of irrigation. In fact some of these modern components have already made a start in Punjab, Haryana, Maharashtra, Gujarat, Himachal Pradesh etc.

4.2 Automated Weather Data Collection and Scheduling

The automated weather data network (AWDN) automatically collects hourly weather measurements. The weather informations can be processed with micro computers and disseminated in nearly real-time basis to farmers and irrigation managers which will help in deciding exact depth, duration and interval of irrigation. The entire scheduling operation can be linked with AWDN and computerised. If such a high level of irrigation management is adopted in live irrigation projects of this country, irrigation personnel as well as irrigators will have to be thoroughly trained in all aspects of such automated scheduling programmes. The state of the art system technologies to be adopted for meeting this country's need shall have to be evolved through relevant research in all concerned aspects.

4.3 Biological Components

There is a scope for a lot of research in biological component such as plant modifications to enhance the ability of plants architecture with biogenetic engineering. Continuous research in this field is need to make it possible for a crop to be grown profitably even in regions and environments unconductive to its growth. This aspect of agricultural subsystem of an irrigation system will have a very important bearing on productivity and irrigation managers as well as farmers will have to be made acquainted with scientific development in this field.

CONCLUSION

There are many disciplines involved in modern irrigation management. Professionals of a particular discipline such as Civil Engineering cannot claim to be efficient and effective irrigation manager unless they receive extensive training in other related inter-disciplinary aspects of land and water management. At the same time indepth continuous research is need to evolve realistic management strategies for an irrigation system. The irrigation managers also need to be acquainted with the emerging new technologies in the field of irrigation management and be constantly and regularly involved in research activities for developing ability to judge the suitability of these technologies for their system. Farmers and beneficiaries also need training in participative management to provide economic sustainability and longevity to the irrigation system.

On the Question of Poverty Eradication

Pradhan H. Prasad

In the India situation, it is a well known fact that there is almost one to one correspondence between alleviation of poverty and eradication of unemployment (including underemployment, disguised unemployment etc.) Unless latter is achieved, the attempt to accomplish the former will be like running after a mirage. It is then a great pity that the different ministries of Government of India, the Planning Commission and a large bulk of academicians are busy estimating the poor population and formulating schemes for them since early sixties. Most of these schemes in their frameworks link poverty alleviation with short term employment generation (including self-employment) but because the main emphasis has been on poverty alleviation in a dependence paradigm rather than on employment growth with a self-reliant ethos, these have remained futile. According to latest estimate of Planning Commission a little less than one-third of Indians are in poverty in 1987-88 and that the percentage of people in poverty has been declining at an annual rate of 2 per cent. On the other hand official figures also suggest that the backlog of unemployment increased from 5.3 million in 1955-56 to 25 million in 1992-93. Among the 33 crores of working men and women today about 24 crores persons include unemployed, disguised unemployment underemployed, and engaged in illegal activities. The concomitant manifestation is found in survival of feudal ethos and identities, low level of consciousness and spurt in activities such as manufacture and trade of spurious goods, drug ped daling, smuggling, dacoities, bank loots, caste and communal violence, ethnic riots, abductions, etc. How this increase in non-development syndrome consistent with the declining poverty ratios or do these ratios carry no meaning? Is there a hope that the nation will ever be able to opt out of this non-development paradigm?

The seventythird amendment of the Constitution of India which was enforced as an Act on April 24, 1993, was greeted by many with optimism. Some of them felt that the country has, though belatedly, taken a step towards achieving the ideals of Gandhi by providing recognition to Gram Sabhas and Panchayats in the Indian Constitution.[1] Is it so? Is it not true that Gandhi lamented the non-inclusion of Panchayati system in the Constitution. It is also true that the young patriots *par excellence* and martyrs to the cause of freedom (1897-1931) known as revolutionaries (some of them drawing inspirations from Marx and Lenin and their doctrine of dictatorship of proletariat) were not averse to the Panchayat system which was deeply rooted in Indian psyche. Ram Prasad Bismil of Kokori fame wrote in his last piece on December 16, 1927. "Hanging has been fixed at 6.30 in the morning of 19th. There is nothing to worry about it. But the grace of God, I shall be re-born many times and my objective shall be to attain complete freedom in the World, everybody shall have equal right on the gift of Nature, so that no one rules over other. Governance by 'Panchayats' shall be universal".[2]

Gandhi, however, was more explicit. His perception about the issues related to the Indian social milieu (saddled with innumerable variations based on caste, creed, race, ethnicity, language, dialects, tradition, culture etc.) prompted him to hypothesis about a fully decentralised form of government in independent India. In 1946, he said, "Independence must begin at the bottom. Thus every village will be a republic or Panchayat having full powers. It follows, therefore, that every village has to be self-sustained and capable of managing its affairs even to the extent of defending itself against the whole world".[3] He further added, " In this structure composed of innumerable villages, there will be everwidening, never ascending circles. Life will be a pyramid with the apex sustained by the bottom. But it will be an oceanic circle whose centre will be the indivudual always ready to perish for the village, the latter ready to perish for the circle of villages, till at last the whole becomes one life composed of individuals, never aggressive in their arrogance but ever humble, sharing the majesty of the oceanic circle of which they are integral units. Therefore, the outermost circumference will not wield power to crush the inner circle but will give strength to all within and derive its own strength from it".[4] The tragedy of Gandhi has been that whatever he perceived and hypothesised during the longdrawn movement against British imperialism (where he not only had a hegemonic role to play but came in contact with millions of poor, exploited and downtrodden), he hardly ever attempted to test the hypotheses by actively involving the millions in the process of 'practice' and thereby failed to promote the raising of understanding and consciousness of the masses in India.[5] This was the undoing of many of his efforts. On many important questions he took a dictatorial attitude.

Often he used to say, he does what God wishes him to do. His whole approach was limited to win the confidence of masses by knowing them intimately.

The seventythird amendment and the legislations following it in the states provide constitutional recognition to a three tier panchayati system in an over centralised form of government ensuring regularity of elections, laying certain conditions for withdrawal of elected office bearers, making provision for reservations of some category of weaker sections of the society and allowing for some additional development work. But except these there is hardly any change worth mentioning in the Panchayati Raj system functioning in India since 1959. Let alone the Government of India, even the panchayats at the district level will not be able to derive strength from the respective Gram Sabhas. On the other hand, as it stands today 'the outmost circumference could wield sufficient power to crush the inner circle'. Thus, the long and rather expensive journey since May 1989 (when the constitutional Amendment Bill on Panchayati Raj was drafted for the first time) till today has brought us to a place which is neither in accordance with the spirit or letter of Gandhi nor that of the revolutionaries. The panchayati system is almost deprived of any autonomy. Still something can be gained out of it.

For example, a people's movement can be launched that the devolution of funds for development works in the panchayati system should first come to Gram Sabhas on per capita basis. It would be the responsibility of the Gram Sabha to decide its needs according to its priorities, how much to keep for itself, how much contribution for the intermediate level and how much for the district level panchayats. For example, a particular Gram Sabha may decide to live with floods rather than have an embankment. Initially, it would mean lengthy negotiated settlement between gram sabhas and panchayats at intermediate and district levels and, therefore, low pace of progress. But then the beneficiary participation and a low pace of progress is certainly better than the existing non-development and dependence paradigm.[6] Moreover, the whole process beginning from the launching of the movement will be geared towards increasing the understanding and raising the consciousness of the masses and activating them. Did not Bhagat Singh who tested the then existing revolutionary theories on Indian soil and courageously embraced matyrdom on March 23, 1931, wrote in the *Manifesto of Revolutionary Programme* (Written in early months of 1931), " The main responsibility of the activists' group of revolutionaries lies in reaching the masses so as to activate them."[7]?

Let us examine yet another possibility. A gram sabha could, in the interest of the unemployed persons (who *ispo facto* are its members), ban the entry of some articles (such as toothpaste, bathing and washing soaps, etc.) in its area either singly or in combination with the neighboring Gram

Sabhas. In this process it could encourage village and household industries and generate employment. If such a phenomenon remains confined to a few pockets, it is likely to be ignored. But if it catches the imagination of the people and spreads to a large area, it will hurt the interests of multinationals, foreign collaborators and their Indian lackeys and finally the interest of the neo-imperialism. The pressure will be mounted to suppress if for the sake of 'free market' commitment. Indian ruling class, in all probability, will succumb, to the pressure. But the problem is, that while all other institutions of the panchayati system can be superseded but not the Gram Sabhas. Their existence shall always be legal and constitutional. How will the struggle proceed, what course will it take, when will it acquire a revolutionary character, all these will depend on the members of the Gram Sabhas. There may be many other possibilities depending on subjective and objective conditions prevailing in different Gram Sabhas. But one thing is certain that along with the struggle (whatever be its form), mass consciousness will increase. This is the lesson which history teaches us and the increasing mass consciousness is the singular need of the hour.

Bhagat Singh and his fellow revolutionaries had not much to fall back upon. They had before them only a few historical facts about revolutionary struggle against imperialism (which has always been the abiding feature of capitalism) such as Sipoy Mutiny of 1857, revolutionary class struggles in France, October Revolution in Russia in 1917, etc. Chartering their course on these meagre perceptions, they plunged themselves in the practice of revolutionary struggle. It was rather very late in the day that they realised the importance of mass consciousness and mass participation in the revolutionary struggle for social justice and progress. This is the central theme in the Manifesto of Revolutionary Programme by Bhagat Singh.[8] History offers many lessons since 1931 and these further re-inforce what is contained as the main theme in the Manifesto.[9]

References

1. The Collected Works of Mahatma Gandhi, Vol. XC, pp. 162 and 217- 8.
2. Singh, Jagmohan and Chamanlal, (ed. 1985), Bhagat Singh Aur Unke sathion Ke Dastawaij (Hindi), Rajkamal Paperbacks 1991, p. 86.
3. Gandhi, M.K., "Independence", Harijan, July 28, 1946, p. 236.
4. Ibid.
5. For example See Prasad, Pradhan H., "Sefl-Reliant Progress Versus Dependence Paradigm", Mainstream, January 29, 1994. p. 36.
6. Ibid.
7. Singh, Jagmohan and Chamanlal, op. cit., p. 403.
8. Ibid. pp. 388-405.
9. Prasad, Pradhan H., (1994), Gandhi, Marx and India, pp. 3-4.

Rural Development, Poverty Alleviation: Linkage with Social Sector Programmes Some Reflections

S.K. Bose

Part-I

(1) Basic Questions

(a) Rural Development and General Economic Development

Before we discuss the implications of rural development, we must not forget that India is still a ruralised country. 70% of the people live in rural areas and 40 to 45 per cent of the National Income is generated in rural areas.

Rural Development therefore in India is not separate from general economic development. The strategy of general economic development of the country is and has to be inclusive of rural development.

Therefore my first submission is that the country in its entirety has first to be considered. If this strategy is well executed it will also bring about development of the rural areas. In other words, rural development is not separate from, but is a part of general economic development.

(2) The Development Model

It used to be said that under Nehru there was neglect of rural development, because of an unrealistic emphasis on industrialisation. From the 2nd plan on wards the emphasis shifted to rapid growth of basic and heavy industries supposed to be based on the So viet model. British and American economists used to comment adversely on this model and this Nehruvian emphasis on basic and heavy industries was supposed to lead to neglect of agriculture. Collapse of the soviet economy has strengthened the criticism that the Soviet path of rapid and heavy industrialisation, blindly imitated by India under the Mahalanobis model, led to the under development of agriculture.

(3) The Controversy Between Agriculture and Industry

As Dr. K.N. Raj pointed out in his lectures delivered in the Nalanda College, Biharsharif 30 years ago, basic industries are basic even for agricultural development.

These basic industries whose development is a pre-condition for agricultural development are Cement, Iron and Steel, Fertilizer and the Chemical Industries producing insectiside and pesticide. and above all power generation.

(4) The above are some of the basic industries which, as every one would admit, are essential for agricultural development in particular and rural development in general. Cement is essential for large scale irrigation projects and even medium and minor projects for lining of channels of canal irrigation. Absence of such cement lining is know to cause wastage of water through seepage and salt effervescence.

Next to water, availability and application of fertilizers is regarded as a basic condition of green revolution.

Even with 45 Years of planned development and the so called misplaced emphasis on fertilizers, the country still remains short of fertilizers. It is sad that the oldest fertilizer plant of the country in Sindri is regarded as a plant which is fit to be abandand, through the latest report indicates that recently it has been earning profits. The Urea Plant in Barauni has remained a sick industry almost right from its inception. The country thus runs short of fertilizers even today and this industry is a basic industry.

Iron and Steel Industry supplies the basic materials for agricultural tools and implements. All sorts of mechanical implements: tractors, harrowers, threshers, harvesters are the products of the machine making industry and industries manufacturing tools. Without a base in Iron and Steel no development of these industries, which are essential for modernisation of agriculture would have been possible.

(5) Power Generation

It used to be thought at one time that power is needed for industrialisation only, and the early development programmes for the power sector used to be pooh-poohed as fanciful. The state Govts. of not only Bihar, but also of

West Bengal are known to have played down programmes of power development, questioning the estimates for demand for power. It is now admitted that the absence of power is not only leading to closure of small scale industries and large scale industries, but what is more significant, power shortage, is holding up proper utilisation of ground water.

It is another matter that excessive tapping of underground water may lead to certain other problems like soil subsidence, as has been warmed by certain geologists.

Power however is necessary even for use in agricultre and irrigation in the form of river pumps, sprinkle irrigation etc.

This is not only for watering crops, power is important for diversifying rural occupations.

The basic reason behind the slow growth of agricultural productivity is said to be excessive population burden on cultivable land. The long term strategy of agricultural development consists of transfer of the surplus population in agricultre to other occupations, not necessarily, to urban areas but even within rural areas. This is because rural industrialisation is now regarded as providing good prospects of employment in non-agricultural rural occupations.

(6) What Should be the Basic Approach to Rural Development

The key to development in any sector, agriculture or industry is improved productivity. In agriculture it should be yield per acre and not so much yield per worker-because land is the scarcest factor.

How yield per acre should improve is well known. Technological and Organisational issues are well known. We have been trying to do it even from before independence. What has been lacking is sustained efforts.

One of the basic defects in our plan procedure has been that the Progress Reports are presented in deliberately ambiguous terminology.

Thus in the first two plan periods progress of projects was presented in terms of the volume of funds expended, not in terms of the physical targets achieved. In such a matter as irrigation the reviews and also sometimes the targets speak of the area "covered", not the area actually irrigated.

As is known to everybody, the Green Revolution, wherever it succeeded, depended crucially on the availability of water.

When the community project idea was presented in the First Five Year Plan, along with the National Extension Service, the Plan document stated that the extension services were the agency, and community project was the idea. The single window approach was said to mark the essence of the Intensive Agricultural District Programme (IADP).

Today we are again hearing of the single window idea. It is nothing new, but may be an admission that in the last 30 years we did not implement this approach properly. We hope that it will be done even now and not remain a topic for discussion in Seminars alone.

After enormous emphasis on the use of synthetic fertilizers, we are being told today by pollution experts of synthetic fertilizer poisoning thc human physiology. The present emphasis is on organic fertilizers. Fifty years ago a movement was started by one Sri N.K. Roy for digging compost pits in villages in which all the refuse and waste matter would be thrown and allowed to ferment, producing highclass organic compost. Gandhiji used to speak of the advantages of dighole latrirnes. They do exist in some places but have not been a common feature.

The Khadi Gramodyog Association has been preaching about the advantages of Gobar Gas, which not only produces energy, but also produces compost from the left over. The Sulabh International Organisation has done yeoman's service in not only sanitation, but energy also.

In short there is no want of ideas, but a miserable failure in their implementation, even after decades.

We have to search for the reasons for such failure. This would take us to the structural and organisational background of Rural Development. In this connection we will briefly review the New Policy regarding Panchayates and the programme for alleviation of poverty and promotion of Rural Employment.

Part-II

Panchayats: Decentralisation and Rural Development.

It was in the late '50s that the Balwant Ray Mehta Committee reported on a de-centralised structure of rural development. It recommended a 3 tier structure for Panchayats. Gram Panchayats at the village level, the Panchayat Samity at the Block level and the Zila Parishad at the District level.

Rural self Government before that was a two tier structure: the local Board at the subdivisional level and the district Board at the district level. Many of our national leaders who subsequently came into power had their first lesson in administration in these institutions.

While the Local Boards did not have much functions to perform other than local roads and outdoor dispensaries the District Board was an important instrument of administration and political apprenticeship. It has construction and maintenance of district level roads, rural water supply, primary education up to the middle level (Middle Schools), and in some places it also took over the running of light railways (Fatuwa-Islampur, the

Bakhtiyarpur-Rajgir and Ara-Sasaram railways were examples).

The Balwant Ray Mehta Committee Report introduced a lower level structure, namely the village panchayats. The village panchayat was not a new concept. It was the traditional un-official instrument of rural self Government. The Balwant Ray Mehta Committee gave it a legal status.

Though the Panchayats did come into being as an organisation in the lowest rung of administration and development, it did not develop very much until recently, except in some states. Not every state adopted the 3 tier structure. Money was released for development work through the official administration. The District Magistrate, subsequently assisted by the District Development Officer, continued to hold the purse strings.

It was with the Jawahar Rojgar Yojana in its 2nd phase that the panchayats at the village level were recognised as developmental agencies, when the Government of India announced that funds from the Centre would come directly to the village Mukhiya. How far it has worked is not known. But according to reports where ever the Mukhiya has been entrusted with the responsibility for executing a development work, there is greater control of the village people over execution of development programmes. After all the Mukhiya is more answerable to the local population than a distant political leader or civil servant.

The recent constitutional amendment has raised the status of the Panchayats. As the Prime Minister stated, while introducing the constitutional amendment, placing Panchayats on a very important pedestal, in many states no election was held to the Panchayats for long years. The present constitutional amendment has been accompanied with the laying down of a time table for the Panchayat elections. Many states have already held the elections.

The question is, even with limited powers, what has been the record of panchayats which came into being after the submission on the Balwant Ray Mehta Committee Report.

Political leaders who realised the potentiality of the panchayats, had wisely decided to capture the Panchayats. The reason why the C.P.M. has been able to continue in power un-interruptedly for more than 17 years is the fact that they captured the majority of the panchayats and made the Panchayats living instruments of power and development. In other States for example in Bihar, the political parties failed to grasp this potentiality; Though there has been a Panchayati structure, both at the official as also the non official level and panchayat conferences have been held from time to time, they were confined to the top level political leaders without a grass-root base. Hence the ruling political parties, what ever their hues, did not hold elections to the Panchayats, nor did they utilise the panchayats as an instrument for mobilising the people.

The Panchayats have been effective instruments of power and development in the states run by Communist Party in West Bengal, Tripura and Kerala, it is in these states where development projects have answered the needs of the people more effectively than in those states where panchayats were not properly utilised.

Land Reforms

India's Land Reforms started long before the transfer of power took place. The objectives of land reforms were:

(1) Providing security of tenure to the tenant.

(2) Protecting the tenant from arbitrary enhancements of rents.

(3) Providing the tenant with transferable rights in respect of his tenancy. These were often described as the goal of 3F' s,e Fair Rent, Fixity of Tenure and Free Transfer.

This process of providing the tenant, i.e, the Man Behind the Plough or the actual tiller of the land, proved to be an elusive pursuit, because of increasing sub-infeudation. Soon after tanacy rights were given to one category of farmers, in course of time he developed into a non-cultivating farmer, with growing population and lack of alternative avenues of employment, land hunger remained a constant factor defeating the goal of land to the tiller.

After independence and abolition of Zamindaries and Intermediaries, efforts were made to protect the crop-sharing tenant also. It is not known how far if this goal has been achieved.

A second element that was added to the programme of land reform was imposition of land ceilings and re-distribution of surplus land. As already noted earlier certain states like West Bengal, Kerala, and Jammu and Kashmir, were known to have implemented the programme of land ceilings and land re-distribution better than other states. It has been in these states that the Panchayati Movement has been more effective, because with legally established land rights the erstwhile crop sharer can now hold his head high. But even these developments have not been able to resolve the problem of poverty and rural unemployment.

Programme for Alleviation of Poverty and of Rural Unemployment

Subject to the remarks made in the beginning of this article, we may briefly review the various programmes under the different plans for Poverty Alleviation and Rural of Employment. At present the most important of these programmes is the Jawahar Rojgar Yojna which is said to coordinate the various programmes under I.R.D.P. i.e. Integrated Rural Development Programme. There was an Employment Programme namely Intensive Rural Employment Programme (I.R.E.P.) which has now been meged with Jawahar Rojgar Yojna. The idea behind these employment programmes was to provide for employment for a minimum number of days in the Year for unemployed youth in rural families. The District Administration under I.R.D.P. and I.R.E.P. was interested in farming and executing programme of development, which aimed at giving employment to rural labour and providing a minimum level of additional income.

There was no well thought out plan for developing the productivity--and thereby the income of rural families. How the additional income supposed to have been generated because of the implementation of the I.R.D.P. schemes was calculated is not clear.

As the Planning Commission remarked in the 7th Five Year, Plan, any permanent improvement in the economic level of a family is possible only through creation of productive assets. In a pre-dominantly agricultural rural family the most important single asset that can add to the income earning capacity of a family is land. For the landless, giving him a piece of land is the most important aspect of Government developmental efforts. For those who are owners of small bits of land. i.e. the marginal and sub-marginal farmers also land is the most important asset which can permanently raise the income earning capacity of a family.

For a rural family with some land, the assets that may enable it to improve productivity are tools and implements, houses, and a few other fixed assets. For meeting the current expenses of cultivation, the small farmer needs credit for purchase of seeds, manures etc that is working capital. In the current programme for Poverty Alleviation the details of how the productivity of the rural family may be improved have not been spelt out. Thus expenditure on improving the income of rural families, which does not bring about any improvement in the capacity of the family to earn more after the programme would then mean merely a re-distribution of money income from the coffers of the Government to the house holds.

Of course I.R.D.P. schemes have also helped construction of Minor Irrigation Projects, Rural Roads and Rural Water Supply.

The measuring rod of all poverty Alleviation Programmes has been the Poverty Line. The Poverty Line concept has been based on a minimum calculated calorific intake, as if fooding is the only relevant element in poverty. The concept of income also has entered into the calculation, based on the assumption of a minimum level of living. The number of days of employment available to the unemployed youth in a family has also been referred to.

It is on these calculations that progress in poverty alleviation has been measured and success claimed. Besides these, there have been some special programmes for the rural landless, for women and children in rural areas. The Rural Landless Employment Guarantee Programme (RLEGP) was supposed to provide guaranteed employment of a 100 days in a year. 25% of these funds was to be devoted to Social Forestry, 10% for works benefiting Scheduled Castes and Scheduled Tribes and 20% for Housing Schemes under the Indira Awas Yojna.

The 8th plan document claims that 115 crores of mandays were generated with an average expenditure of Rs. 21 per manday. This figure is just a little below the minimum rural wage fixed under the Minimum Wages Act. It is not known how far a 100 days of employment at Rs. 21 per day will have made any contribution to alleviation of poverty and improvement in levels of living.

Other Programmes

Other programmes for rural Development comprise Drought Prone Area Programme, Social Forestry Programme, Land Development Programme and Water Resources Development Programme.

The 8th plan document says that the organisations of beneficiaries of Anti-Poverty Programmes were intended to increase the awareness and strengthen the bargaining position of the beneficiaries of these programmes so as to help them get the maximum benefits from all Governmental programmes meant for them.

The Council of Advancement of People's Action and Rural Technology has been set up for providing and assisting voluntary action in the area of Rural Development.

It is in this connection that mention may be made of TRYSEM, i.e. Training of Rural Youth for Self Employment.

The Planning Commission admits in the 8th Plan document that while Poverty Alleviation Programmes have been successful in providing a certain quantum of some durable assets in the village, there is a perception that the achievements have not been commensurate with the resources spent on them. The fact that advances given are not being repaid proves that they are not able to come out of the debt syndrome. Low level assistance fails to bring about any substantial increase in income that would enable them to repay the loans and have a permanent increase in their income. The Planning Commission notes that Banks are reluctant to raise the credit level. The Commission also admits that the wages earned under JRY are a very small proportion of the amount required to help the poor to cross the Poverty Line. Very often the schemes taken up do not reflect the priorities of the local people and even when executed are not properly maintained.

Concluding Observations

The above rather long review of efforts made for improving the rural economy leads us to the conclusion that the efforts made so far have failed to bring about any substantial improvement in the levels of living in rural areas. The basic handicap is that limited resources have been spread over a large area.

- Poverty has been sought to be reduced by providing employment for a 100 days in the Year, generating income, which if spread over the whole year will hardly make any impact on the level of living.

As remarked in the beginning, creation of employment through these projects is bound to fail, unless the employment created is sustained on a more permanent basis.

Specific programmes like Drought Prone Area Development or land reclamation projects are good, but can not be applied to the whole country. If land reforms were pushed to the logical end, some permanent employment could have been created by more intensive cultivation of the land.

Income disparities have been aggravated because effective land reforms have not taken place. Co-operatives, particularly, co-operative farming, has failed, because cooperation can succeed only amongst equals.

Therefore for removing rural poverty and raising the levels of living efforts for expanding production through providing more irrigation, construction of roads and provision of electricity are more important than any so called direct attacks on poverty.

Poverty Alleviation Programmes Status, Impediments and Remedies

M.K. Aggarwal

During the last decades, with the planned development, the country's economy has been modernised and now liberalised and made self-reliant. Of course, the standard of living of the people has improved and there is also a modest rate of growth in per capita income but there has not been noticed any significant change in the poverty of the people as still more that 30% of the population is living below the poverty line. During the year 1979-80, the Planning Commission, in a study, estimated about 48.13% of the population living below the poverty line. Different studies established the fact that the poverty is the direct result of our socio-economic circumstances prevailing in the society. One major problem i.e. unemployment is also closely associated with the problem of poverty. It can be said that the poverty and unemployment are two major problems of our country. Both these problems are so closely associated that one can not be separated from the other. As such, it was felt that by solving one problem, the other would also be solved quite substantially. As such removal of poverty has been central concern of planning in India. While formulating the plans to combat poverty, it was felt that unless a direct attack on poverty is launched by identification of the members of 'target group' and providing assistance to them in terms of subsidy, credit, inputs and marketing facilities etc., the development efforts would not alleviate poverty.

During the 4th-5th Five Year Plan, special attention was given by the Government to poverty alleviation, particularly rural poverty. Special Programmes were introduced for the benefit of the poor relatively less privileged classed and backward areas. Beneficiary-oriented programmes like SFDA (Small Farmers Development Agency), MFAL (Marginal Farmers and Agricultural Labourers Agency) etc. aimed at helping the specific target group of beneficiaries, were started. Further, a review of various ongoing Special Programmes of Rural Development taken up, indicated the need for a new and comprehensive programme for development of rurals mass. Thus, the Integrated Rural Development Programme came into being in 1978-79 with the objective of taking up families in the identified target groups below the poverty line and creating substantial additional opportunities for employment in rural areas. The target group consists of the poorest among the poor in rural areas i.e. small farmers, marginal farmers, agricultural and non-agricultural labourers, rural artisans and craftsman, scheduled castes and scheduled tribes.

As the main focus is on taking families below the poverty line, the basic crieterion to be used for indentifying the family, is the income of the family which is presently Rs. 11,000/- per annum or less from all sources. In this programme, the Bank's role was to provide the credit to the beneficiary identified. While providing financial assistance by the bank to the identified beneficiaries, the expectations were:

(i) Through the financial assistance to beneficiaries to their selected schemes, there should be increase in income.
(ii) New employment opportunities should be created through each financial assistance.
(iii) There should be increase in income through the loans provided for the schemes.
(iv) The repayment of loans should be out of the income generated from schemes.

IRDP, the main poverty alleviation programme thus, was launched in 1978-79 in 2300 selected blocks all-over the country and later it was extended to all the development blocks of the country since 2nd October 1980. Since then about 422 lakhs families have so far been provided the financial assistance by the financial agencies in the country and a total of Rs. 18,728.30 crores have so far been spent on the programme. During the 8th plan also the Government plans to help 1.26 crores families through this programme. Since, the IRDP came into being, year after year resources were being deployed for the benefit of the designated 'poor' and it is a fact that only 13% of the population below the poverty line was able to cross over the same. The financial institutions have been providing financial assistance to the extent of 75% and 66.2/3% of the total cost of pre-set schemes like dairy, poultry, fishers, sheep and goat rearing, cycle repairing, petty trade, bullock cart, calf rearing etc.

At one time, in pre-nationalisation of Banks period (1969) credit markets were inaccessible for the poor. Today through direct intervention by the Government, the credit markets are thrown open to the poor. But the risks attached to these to credit markets have not been brought down.

Today the sizeable amount of loans under IRDP have been provided by the financial institutions and substantial part of these loans have become bad, their recovery is very low. The State Bank of India, Patna Circle participated in the programme enthusiastically and invested as much as Rs. 258.01 crores spread over 9.27 lack beneficiaries. But, for the reasons enumerated below the recovery of bank loans remained very low (16.46%). The economic liberalisation cupled with introduction of various prudential norms have compelled the banks to concentrate on recovery of loans as well so that they are not deprived of the interest earning on the one hand and can avoid making provisions out of the profit, on the other. The large scale non-recovery of loans under IRDP is a consequence of number of reasons:

(i) The beneficiaries were given the impression that the loans were meant to be written off and therefore, need not bother about the utility.
(ii) No marketing arrangements were made for the produce.
(iii) The identification of beneficiaries and selection of activity were left on the mercy of Village Level Worker.
(iv) The financing agencies were not associated at the time of selection of beneficiaries and selection of activities.
(v) In the anxiety of achieving the target, due time/attention was not given to the basic inputs before sponsoring the loan application to the bank.
(vi) Impact of ARDR have also vitated the climate of recovery of loans.
(vii) Absence of backward and forwarded linkages.

Thus, it is apparent that under the name of directed lending there has been almost a complete erosion in the banking discipline in respect of loans under IRDP. Therefore, thrust of such programmes require a new direction and approach. In essence, the time is ripe now for innovation of our strategies. Innovations like formation/ promotion of self help groups to infuse greater co-operation and eventual responsibility can not be ruled out. The borrowing units in the changed circumstance will have to observe greater financial discipline and commercial sense to be able to compete and prosper rather than living and being looked upon with as a subject of sympathy.

In the light of the above, we are suggesting the following remedial measures for successful implementation of the on-going programme of IRDP.

(i) A master list of all the beneficiaries should be prepared at one attempt for all the villages in a block and bankers should identify and verify the families and area specific projects suitable for them for financing under the programme.

(ii) Government should undertake to promote marketing societies for the marketing of the produce.

(iii) Cluster approach for the activity selected should be implemented so that the programme should be implemented areawise and activitywise.

(iv) A distinction should be made between two categories of poor, those who posses some skill and those who are not having any skill. In the first category, the beneficiaries should come under IRDP and in 2nd category, the beneficiaries should be provided employment under Jawahar Rojgar Yojna.

(v) Eligibility criteria for selection of beneficiaries should also include--

 (a) Beneficiaries above 60 years of age should be made ineligible.

 (b) Those who are defaulters earlier should also be ineligible.

 (c) The close kin living under the same roof of the defaulter should be ineligible.

(vi) Absconders should be dealt with sternly and Banks suits should not be on par with civil suits with elongated procedures.

(vii) Effective and stem action should be taken in the case of misutilisation of loans.

(viii) There should be stature that no loans shall be waived in future.

(ix) The borrowers have to be given a clear message that they should try to gradually reduce their dependence either on the government or on financial institution by achieving a self-sustaining growth.

Through the implementation of these programmes, the country is moving towards better economy. As the process of economic development is a continuous one, a poor and developing country like ours has to march a long way ahead for attaining the desired level of economic development. Being a Welfare estate, India's economic development is always tagged with "Social Justice". No doubt, through the implementation of the poverty alleviation programmes, we have achieved our goal to some extent but still a long distance is to be covered. The Banking institutions are participating enthusiastically in the implementation of these programmes and intend to continue it, but their profit is being eroded by incurring loss through implementation of such programmes. At this juncture, it is felt, the Banking institution needs the support from the Government to enable them to keep up the enthusiasm to participate in the poverty-alleviation programmes in future.

Poverty, Programmes and People

H.K. Sinha

Poverty line is a line which divides the poor from non-poor by putting a price on the minimum required consumption levels of food, clothing, shelter, fuel and health care etc. In a seminar on "Some Aspects of Planning" it was decided to setup a working group to define the concept of poverty line. A working group was therefore, set up which comprised eminent economists and social thinkers like Prof. D.R. Gadgil, Dr. B.N. Ganguli, Dr. P.S. Loknathan, Shri M.R. Masani, Shri Ashok Mehta, Shri Pitambar Pant, Dr. V.K.R.V. Rao, Shri Sriman Narayan and Shri Anna Saheb Sahasrabuddhe. After sufficient discussion on minimum standard of living and taking into account the recommendations of the Nutrition Advisory Committee of the Indian Council of Medical Research (ICMR) regarding balanced diet, this working group recommended in 1962 that:

(i) The national minimum for each household of 5 persons (4 adult consumption units) should be not less than Rs. 100/- per month in terms of 1960-61 prices or Rs. 20/- per capita. For urban areas, this figure will have to be raised to Rs. 125/- per month for household or Rs. 25/- per capita to cover the higher prices of the physical volume of commodities on which the national minimum is calculated.

(ii) This national minimum excludes expenditure on health and education, both of which are expected to be provided by the State according to the constitution and in the light of other Commitments.

(iii) An element of subsidy in urban housing will have to be included after taking Rs. 10/- per month, or 10 per cent as the rent element payable from the national minimum of Rs. 100/- per month.

2. However on the basis of National Sample Survey data on consumption and using an average calorie norm of 225 calories per capita per day for both rural and urban areas, Dandekar and Rath defined poverty line at 1960-61 price Rs. 170.80 for rural areas and Rs. 271.70 for urban area. They later decided to put the poverty line at Rs. 180/- per annum or Rs. 15/ - per month for rural area and Rs. 270/- per annum or Rs. 22.50 per month for urban areas.

3. But 1962 working group recommendation of poverty line was made use of by the Planning Commission in all its inter State and other considerations which had an element of poverty ratio.

4. In January 1979, the "Task Force on Projection of Minimum Needs and Effective Consumption Demand" of Perspective Planning Division formulated a methodology by incorporating various studies of seventies relating to poverty line conception. Accordingly, this Task Force defined poverty line as the per capita expenditure level at which the average per capita, per day calorie intake was 2435 calories in rural areas and 2095 calories for urban areas. For sake of arithmetical conveniences, the calories intake for rural areas and urban areas were rounded off at 2400 and 2100 respectively. The monetary equivalent to these norms were derived on the basis on 28th Round (1973-74) on NSS data relating to household consumption both in quantity and value.

Based on observed consumer behaviour, the poverty line for 1973-74 was defined for Rural areas at Rs. 49.09 per capita per month and Rs. 56.64 per capita per month for Urban areas by this Task Force. Accordingly after using private consumption deflator derived from National Accounts Statistics, the poverty line for the years 1977-78, 1973-84 were projected by the Planning Commission both for the nation as well as for the states.

5. However, such estimates suffered from the fact that the poverty line, so defined was anchored in a norm of calorie requirement which did not seek to measure nutritional status, incidence of malnourishment or under nourishment in the population.

6. With an end to avoid this lacuna, Planning Commission constituted in September 1989 an Expert Group to "look into the methodology for estimation of poverty at national and state level and also to go into the question of redefining poverty line, if necessary". This group comprised Professor D.T. Lakdawalla (Chairman), Prof. V.M. Dandekar, Prof. B.S. Minhas, Prof. P.V. Sukhatame, Dr. R. Radhakrishnan, Dr. A. Vaidyanathan, Shri S.A. Guhan, Prof. Suresh D. Tendulkar, Director General C.S.O. Chief Executive Officer

NSSO and Prof. S.R. Hashim, Adviser Perspective Plan Division, Planning Commission. Dr. Raja Chelliah, Dr. Yogendra K. Alagh, were also members of this group at the initial stage.

7. This expert group after many deliberations and considerable studies, has recommended that--

(i) The poverty line of Rs. 49.09 or Rs. 50 (rural) and Rs. 56.64 or Rs. 57 (Urban) at all India level at 1973-74 be adopted as the base line and uniformly adopted for all states ie. the poverty line approach anchored in a caloric norm and associated with a fixed consumption basket may be continued.

(ii) State specific poverty line should be estimated by price adjustment for inter-state variations in the base year and State specific price movements over time.

(iii) Suitable and representative deflators should be used to arrive at the State specific poverty line.

8. Using the new methodology this expert group arrived at new percentage of poor and non-poor for states and the country and it recommended that the new estimates for 1973-74, 1978-79, 1983 and 1987 should replace the earlier estimates officially released by the Planning Commission.

9. Thus the old and new poverty ratio for the country and Bihar, M.P. U.P. and West Bengal, Orissa, Rajasathan are as follows:

Combined Percent of Population Below Poverty Line

	1973-74		1977-78		1983		1987-88	
	Old	New	Old	New	Old	New	Old	New
	(1972-73)				(1983-84)			
Bihar	54.5	61.78	56.3	61.95	49.5	62.51	40.8	53.37
M.P.	58.6	61.90	58.9	62.43	46.2	50.13	36.7	43.40
U.P.	52.8	56.98	49.7	49.19	45.3	47.19	35.1	41.99
W.B.	56.8	63.39	52.2	60.65	39.2	54.72	27.6	43.99
Orissa	68.6	66.24	65.1	70.35	42.8	65.32	44.7	55.63
Rajasth.	46.0	46.33	33.6	37.99	34.3	35.02	24.4	34.60
Mahar.	47.7	52.54	50.6	56.06	34.9	43.54	29.2	40.10
All India	51.5	54.93	48.3	51.88	37.4	44.76	29.9	39.34

On the latest estimate of population below poverty line, the % reduction in poverty in these states between 1973 to 1987 i.e, 14 years have been as follow:-

Bihar	-	8.41
Madhya Pradesh	-	18.50
Uttar Pradesh	-	14.99
West Bengal	-	19.40
Orissa	-	10.63
Rajasthan	-	11.73
Maharastra	-	15.96
All India	-	15.59

10. This indicates that Bihar's effort to bridge the gulf between poor and non-poor has been poorest in the country. The number of persons below poverty line as per the new estimates in these states are:--

No. of Persons Below Poverty Line

(Figure in lac)

Increase /decrease in 14 years.	Name of the State	1973-74	1977-78	1983-84	1987-88
1.	2.	3.	4.	5.	6.
+ 70.05	Bihar	369.79	404.43	465.95	439.84
(-) 10.95	Madhya Pradesh	276.84	306.05	279.38	265.8[illegible]
+ 2.19	Uttar Pradesh	534.86	505.83	557.54	537.05
(-) 22.38	West Bengal	299.10	311.24	317.10	276.72
+ 13.34	Orissa	154.62	177.03	181.79	167.96
+ 12.15	Rajasthan	129.04	118.64	130.28	141.19
+ 8.35	Maharashtra	285.83	330.96	291.79	294.18
+ 88.55	All India	3216.03	3319.08	3270.08	3127.48

Thus taking into consideration the rise in population between 1973 to 1987, in absolute numbers also the population of poor in the country has been reduced by nearly nine million but in Bihar it has increased by seven million. With this kind of performance to alleviating poverty in this State and with the current rate of population growth, the subsequent estimates after 1987 would further increase the number of poor people amongst us as compared to our neighboring States as well as the country as a whole.

11. Another startling feature of the recent estimate of poverty line indicates that in Bihar poverty ratio for urban area is higher than that of its rural area. It indicates that in 1987-88 in urban areas of this State the percentage of poor people is 57.71 as against 52.63 per cent in rural area. This was not the picture for 1983 wherein rural areas had 64.37% rural population below poverty line and the poor in urban areas accounted for only 50.42 per cent. Thus in 4 (four) years period while there has been reduction in percentage of poor people in rural areas by 11.74 per cent, poor people's percentage in urban areas has increased by 7.29 percent. The recent estimates also indicates that number of poor persons in Rural areas had decreased from 415.90 lakhs to 370.36 lakh in 4 years period i.e. 45.54 lakh persons were made to cross poverty line in this period, whereas in urban areas poor persons increased from 50.05 lakh to 69.48 lakh i.e. additional 19.43 lakh persons residing in urban area of this State became poor and were thrown to a life of living in malnourishment, ill clothing and ill healthy conditions.

12. However, like Bihar, States like Andhra Pradesh, Goa, Gujrat, Karnataka, Kerala, Madhya Pradesh, Punjab, Rajasthan and Uttar Pradesh have also shown increased percentage of poor in urban areas as compared to their rural areas. The position is as follows:--

No. of Persons Below Poverty Line in Urban Areas

	1987-88 % of poor Persons in Rural areas	% of poor Persons in Urban areas	No. of poor 1983 (Lakhs)	1987-88 (Lakhs)	Increase/ Decrease in Poor persons in urban areas. (Lakhs)
	1.	2.	3.	4.	5.
A.P.	20.92	44.63	56.07	72.88	16.81
Bihar	52.63	57.71	50.05	69.48	19.43
Goa	17.64	33.71	1.09	1.42	0.33
Gujarat	28.67	39.63	47.26	52.63	5.37
Karnataka	32.82	49.06	52.31	68.39	16.08
Kerala	29.10	43.36	25.61	26.02	00.39
M.P.	41.92	48.17	65.85	70.04	4.19
Punjab	12.60	12.91	12.37	7.77	(-) 4.60
Rajasthan	33.21	38.99	33.31	38.17	4.86
U.P.	41.10	45.22	114.78	125.02	11.24
All India	39.06	40.12	752.93	833.52	80.59

Bihar accounts for highest increase in number of poor people in urban areas in the country. The increase can be attributed to migration of poor people in search of job in urban areas where also the avenues of fresh employment has not been commensurate to absorb the migrants. Deterioration in law and order in rural areas might also account for migration of rural poor to urban areas.

13. It indicates that our effort towards poverty alleviation is mismatch to the rise in population and that unless population is controlled and concrete steps for the increasing the development index like educational facilities, public health programme coupled with increase in avenues of employment facilities are taken, problem of poverty alleviation in Bihar will become insurmountable. A sort of preventive efforts to outmatch this growing Herculian task involves increased investment in free education specially to all girl child, reduction in dropout in schools and motivated appraoch to enhance the availability of public health facilities at the door step of poor.

14. The education of girls has been more powerful determinants of falling family size. There is a Jamaican saying, "those who feel it know it". The oppression of large destitute family is really felt by women. 'Educate the female child' should be the slogan of the present time. Monetary investment is not all that matters. Close link between the parent and the teacher is necessary. It is good that we are planning for investment of 6% GNP in Education from Ninth Five Year Plan. But education for all by 2000 AD, there is really not aimed at. If Sri Lanka and Zimbabwe both having per capita GNP of less than $600 can provide 90 per cent of their children with at least four years of primary schools, we can also do it provided we avoid our wastages. This is high time to denationalise all the primary schools and use this money in giving incentive to such private individuals, institutions communities who wish to run free educational facilities for their girl children. Recently U.P. has taken a decision in this direction. The fall out of the 73rd constitutional amendment is control of primary education by Panchayats. Instead of giving absentee teacher primary schools to Panchayats, it is better to transfer proportionate money to Panchayats from the money saved after denationalisation of existing primary schools. Village Primary Schools should largely have locally available educated females as teacher who would neither resent on transfer nor would absent from duties. The scarce monetary resources of the state can be used judiciously and pragmatically to atleast achieve education for all female child by 2000 AD if earnest effort is done. The late D.P. Dhar Vice-Chairman of Planning Commission had termed nationalisation of our primary schools sarcastically as "Shagufa".

15. Public health care facilities can be made to reach the poor, if village level cadres and not imported ladies like those working on existing aganbadis ICDS and primary, health schemes run these programmes. Locally available educated, semi-educated or skilled ladies in the village or those available within a radius of 2 kms. can be entrusted to run public health programmes at the door step of the poor. Removal of consumption of non-iodidsed salt, immunisation and oral rehydration therapy can create wonders towards public health programme. Media must help in propagating advantage of use of iodised salt, ORS and immunisation. Efforts in this direction have been accentuated but the task is enormous which can be accomplished by involving voluntary agencies functioning at the Pacnchayat level. It is reported that our state has achieved the target of providing safe drinking water facility in each village. All problematic villages indentified as per 1981 census and later identified in 1985 have been convered by safe drinking water facility by 1992-93. Such official report might not be entirely true, but for sake of containing water borne diseases, it is essential that fresh survey is made out quickly because money is available under the rural development programmes for investment under this scheme. Not only regular survey for providing safe drinking water facilities in villages but for maintenance of available resources should be got done by each Panchayat who would have effective control over them under the Panchayati Raj Act.

16. Providing wage employment to the rural poor for bringing down the percentage of people below the poverty line is an integral part of programme like JRY. The primary objective of JRY is "generation of additional gainful employment for the unemployed and under-employed, men and women, in rural areas" and the first among five secondary objectives is 'creation of sustained employment by strengthening the rural economic infrastructure". "Positive impact on wage level" is another secondary objective. However GOI report indicates that only 64 per cent of the fund made available under JRY could be utilised till November, 93. in our state such pitfalls can now be better handled by Panchayats which have been duly empowered.

17. Bihar however, appears to be unconcerned with magnitude of the task involved in poverty alleviation. Under the Integrated Rural Development Programme, poverty line is drawn at an annual income level of Rs. 11,000, however the assistance under IRDP is tagetted at the rural families having an annual income below a cut off line of annual family income of Rs. 8,500. Among these families with annual income upto Rs. 6400 are assisted first. This requires a survey of the families in the villages and Panchayats. This does not appear to have been done as yet. It is why unlike other states (except J and K) Bihar is unable to report the coverage of old and new families separately under this programme. The first evaluation of IRDP conducted by Planning Commission in 1983-84 had reported that no house hold survey was done in this state. This resulted in wrong selection and identification of beneficiaries. Reserve Bank of India had also done field study of the utlisation of loans under the scheme for self-employment to educated unemployed youth for the year 1983-84 and 1984-85. R.B. I's finding had also indicated wrong identification of beneficiaries. The Annual Report 1993-94 of the Rural Development Ministry has again indicated that evaluation studies carried out by RBI, NABARD, Institute of Financial Management and Research and the Programme Evaluation Organisation of Planning Commission have found "shortcomings in regard to the selection of beneficiaries, low level of investment, lack of infrastructure and linkages". By not holding the household survey before embarking upon the implementation of programme, avenues for leakage, wastage and nonfulfillment of the target get created from the beginning. The survey of beneficiaries under the IRDP programme must be done and completed quickly.

18. Earnest implementation of TRYSEM and Nehru Rojgar Yojna can help create not only opportunities for self employment but avenues of gainful employment also. However, record of performance of TRYSEM scheme in Bihar is much below the national average and is also lowest in the country as per annual report 1993-94. Bihar could train hardly 19% of rural youth as against 94% by Haryana, 32% by Rajasthan, 34% by Madhya Pradesh, 28% by Uttar Pradesh and 30% by West Bengal through this scheme.

19. Our record of success in the women's programme namely DWCRA (development of women and children in Rural areas) is also not heartening. This scheme gets implemented in fattening of Bank deposits rather than developing women and children in rural areas. It has no linkage with programmes like ICDS, Anganwari, public health care programmes. Instead of keeping Rs. 15,000 under each Panchayat through bank deposits in various banks, if all panchayats pool their amount and keep it deposited at one Bank, this scheme can be more fruitfully implemented. Interest earned from this amount can be utilised in locating and initiating locally available educated girls in villages who could move and motivate the village women more fruitfully to generating avenues of self employment through real exploitation of available skills suitably moulded by proper training.

20. For creating assured employment facilities for 100 days to poor and needy, in rural areas, Employment Assurance Scheme (EAS) is being implemented from October, 1993 in 1752 blocks of 257 districts in which the Revamped Public Distribution System (RPDS) is in operation. Recently Government of India has taken decision to implement in additional 500 blocks of the country.

The EAS is presently being implemented in 157 blocks of 14 Districts of this state. Obviously this scheme has to reach such blocks/ Districts which have largest concentration of poor people. Per capita income is best yardstick to measure this requirement in absence of district wise poverty line data. The Directorate of Economics and Statistics, Bihar has calculated the per capita income of each district of Bihar for 1990-91 and has brought out a booklet also. The fourteen districts which rank poorest interse are given below besides the fourteen districts where this scheme is under execution:-

Sl. No	Per capita Income (of District) rank lowest from below (Rs)	Name of the District having Col. (2)	Name of the District where EAS is implemented
1.	2.	3.	4.
1.	1460	Aararia	Rohtas
2.	1680	Saran	Bhabhua
3.	1702	Godda	Nawadah
4.	1730	Khagaria	Jamui
5.	1782	Vaishali	Dumka
6.	1796	Darbhanga	Sahibganj
7.	1828	Sitamarhi	Godda
8.	1841	Samastipur	Ranchi
9.	1912	Jehanabad	Lohardagga
10.	1913	Saharsa	Gumla
11.	1923	Nawadah	East Singhbhum
12.	1924	Begusarai	West Singhbhum
13.	1955	Gaya	Palamu
14.	1956	Katihar	Garhwa
15.	1982	Purnea	"
16.	2005	East Champaran	"
17.	2011	Nalanda	"
18.	2022	Siwan	"
19.	2034	Madhubani	"
20.	2052	Munger	"

Again a question of wrong identification of district and of beneficiaries become apparent in the execution of EAS as well as RPDS in our State. Eighty per cent outlay of this scheme is met by central government. Performance of this scheme is disheartening in as much as during 1993-94, against released amount of Rs. 5880 lakh, Bihar could spend only 1608. 76 i.e. hardly 28 per cent of the available fund in the implementation of this scheme. As against 8766 projects initiated under this scheme, only 507 i.e. hardly 6 per cent programmes could be completed. This being an employment assurance scheme for 100 days, only such project should have been taken up after October 93 which could have been completed latest by February, 94. This indicates that large projects being mismatch with the intention of EAS have been taken up for execution in this state. This calls for immediate review to ensure stoppage of wastage and employment of 100 days to 2 adults of each needy rural poor family through execution of this scheme.

21. Another important scheme which could change the face of poverty in concerned rural areas is the Drought Prone Area Programme. This scheme is being implemented as follows:

Sl. No	District	Blocks
1	Palamau	16
2	Garhwa	8

{Cont}		
3	Godda	8
4	Jamui	7
5	Nawadah	9
6	Bhabhua	5
7	Rohtas	2
		55

DPAP is a centrally sponsored scheme having State share of 50% of the outlay. State could not give its matching share in 1993-94 nor did it utilise the full fund released by the Centre. Its progress has been as follows:--

(Rs. in lakhs)

Year	Allocation	Expenditure	% of Execution
1985-90	3924.00	4329.28	110.23
1990-91	828.00	669.97	80.43
1991-92	828.00	568.45	68.29
1992-93	828.00	579.51	69.99
1993-94	1242.00	880.28	70.88

22. Inter and intra caste fight has adversely affected the pace of rural development. People, instead of garnering community spirit in furtherance of the interest of their habitats, villages and panchayat forcibly cut the harvest, do not allow sowing of seeds, compel withdrawal of labourers from paddy field and create situation where in the agriculturists prefer to allow their land to remain fallow instead of sowing seeds of trouble for themselves and their children. Peace appears to have been snatched away either in name of caste, rangdari or forcible illegal occupation and uncultivated harvest. Eventually the sufferance is more for those who create troubles. Those who in the name of forcible occupation of surplus land take law into their own hand, succeed only in depriving cultivation of the land. Such village rangdars are saddist by temperament who easily sway away the poor peasants and agricultural labours by giving false alluration of getting such lands transferred to them. The agriculturists largely decide in favour of buying temporary peace and keep the land uncultivated. In this process, the agricultural labour are forced to leave the village for employment elsewhere, because they neither get the promised land nor the traditional source of employment to sustain themselves.

23. There is irrefutable evidence of cultivable lands having been allowed to remain fallow in such places. Statistics reveal that total operational holding in Bihar which was 114.8 lakh hectors in 1970-71, got reduced to 110.7 lakh hectors in 1980-81 and it further came down to 102.4 lakh hectors in 1980-90. Thus in a period of about twenty years the fall in operational holding was 12.4 lakh hectors. The net area sown during 1970-71 stood at

84,54,000 hectors, but it went down to 83,15,000 during 1980-81 and further dropped to 77,25,000 hectors in 1989-90 i.e., 7,29,000 hectors could not be cultivated in this period because of village *ashanti*. Bihar had 14.1 per cent of area as fallow land, in 1970-71 but this increased to 15.3% during 1980-81 and to 16.2% in 1989-90. This has adversely affected the States' foodgrain out put as well. Bihar which contributed 8.46 per cent towards total foodgrain output of the country during 1970-73 triennia could contribute only 6.68% of national foodgrain output during 1989-90 triennia period. In Bihar per capita foodgrain production which was 155 Kg. in the 1970-73 triennia, became as low as 121 kg. in 1980-83 and which improved to only 133 kg. during 1989-90 triennia. The per capita rural income from agriculture in Bihar during 1986-89 triennia stood at Rs. 943 which was 72 per cent of the national average of Rs. 1302 and was only 85 per cent of the average income of Rs. 1104 of the other poor states comprising U.P., M.P., Orissa and Rajasthan. Had there been no increase in fallow land and no decrease in net sown area during this period, Bihar's economy could have given better result because even with fall in sown area, the total production of foodgrains rose to 114,49,000 tons in 1989-92 period from 87,57,000 tons in 1970-73 period.

24. Some protagonists of the theory of achieving forcible land occupation may argue that other states like Tamil Nadu and Gujarat have also shown reduction in net sown area during this period. The fact, however, is that except Bihar, those state's fall in net sown area resulted from change over from foodgrain to non-foodgrain crops and are not due to the causes which attributed such fall of cultivation in Bihar. The figures are as follows:-- (See table 'A' on next page).

25. Bihar's rural economy has, therefore, suffered from the hands of those who lack comprehension in asking illiterate and starving agricultural labours to shy away from tilling the agriculturist's land and to forcibly occupy and harvest produces of such land which do not belong to them. These incidents were few and far between during sixties but has increased manifold during eighties and nineties. This have resulted in migration of agricultural labour and increase in fallow land and decrease in production and in rural income. These illegal measures are superficially initiated as forcible implementation of land reforms which could not be legally implemented by Government in Bihar. But statistics has other story to tell. The surplus land distribution in Bihar is better than that of Kerala and Madhya Pradesh. The land possession rate of surplus distributed land in Bihar is also much better than Kerala. The figures are as follows:- (See table 'B' on next page).

Table 'A' : States Showing fall in Net Sown Area during 1970-90

States	Net shown area 000 hects			Food crop (Lakh Hetcs)			Non-food crop (Lakh Hetcs)		
	1970-71	1980-81	1989-90	1970-71	1980-81	1989-90	1970-71	1980-81	1989-90
Andhra Pradesh	11735	10733	11094	94.9	87.6	80.5	32.8	30.2	47.7
Bihar	8454	8315	7725	99.1	100.2	94.2	7.6	8.3	7.5
Gujarat	9713	9517	7231	51.0	44.7	47.3	38.9	44.7	40.4
Tamil Nadu	6169	5360	5662	52.0	41.1	43.3	19.1	17.4	20.4
Uttar Pradesh	17305	17221	17232	196.3	204.7	203.8	56.1	57.7	45.1
West Bengal	5462	5565	5334	61.2	61.0	63.4	7.7	14.2	8.2

Table 'B' : The Land Possession Rate of Surplus Distributed Land in Bihar

(Figures-June 1992' 000 hect)

States	Land declared surplus	Land taken possession	Land distributed	Land under litigation as on 31.3.92	Land possession rate% col (2)/ col (1)	Land distri-bution rate% of .3/ col (2)	% of surplus land under litigation col (4)/col.(1)
	(1)	(2)	(3)	(4)	(5)	(6)	(7)
Bihar	192.2	160.3	112.1	45.0	83.40	69.93	23.4
Kerala	54.6	37.6	25.9	10.0	68.86	68.88	18.3
M.P.	129.9	113.3	74.1	22.6	85.68	66.58	17.4
Orissa	70.0	65.6	60.3	5.9	93.71	91.92	8.4
Uttar Pradesh	217.7	204.8	147.3	21.3	94.64	77.95	13.9
West Bengal	513.5	486.0	378.8	71.4	94.64	77.95	13.9
All India	2946.4	2571.0	2013.3	440.5	87.26	78.31	15.0

Certain litigations in taking possession of surplus land are bound to exist and other states like Kerala and West Bengal have also this problem. It does help no body to take law in one's possession to forcibly occupy the surplus land. Rural Development is the real casualty in such illegal and forcible measures, since in absence of rule of law, development is bound to get eclipsed.

26. Rural people, therefore, has greater role to play in getting things sorted out through negotiations and democratic means. Poverty, hunger and starvation thrive in zones where absence of rule of law prevails. This is being witnessed in districts of Central Bihar. A news item published in Hindustan dated 16.10.94. is quoted below (The name of the political party and concerned Sena have been purposely omitted).

पुनपुन थानान्तर्गत पारथू गांव में खेत जोतने के प्रश्न पर किसान एवं राजनैतिक दल के कार्यकर्त्ताओं के बीच उत्पन्न तनाव हो जाने के कारण दोनों ओर से करीब पचास राउंड गोली चलने का समाचार मिला है। पारथू गांव में तैनात पुलिसकर्मियों को आत्मरक्षार्थ तीन राउंड गोली चलानी पड़ी।

बताया जाता है कि राजनैतिक दल के कार्यकर्त्ताओं ने पारथू गांव के करीब बीस एकड़ जमीन पर खेती करने पर पाबन्दी लगा दी थी। पुलिस के अनुसार कल ही पारथू गांव के किसान ट्रेक्टर से विवादित जमीन को जोत रहे थे कि राजनैतिक दल कार्यकर्त्ताओं ने खेत जोतने से उन्हें मना किया। तत्पश्चात् किसान एवं राजनैतिक दल के कार्यकर्त्ता जो पूर्व से सशस्त्र तैयार थे एक दूसरे पर गोली की बौछार करने लगे। राजनैतिक दल के कार्यकर्त्ताओं ने गांव में तैनात पुलिस कर्मियों पर भी गोली चलाई, जिसके जवाब में पुलिस कर्मियों ने आत्मरक्षार्थ तीन राउन्ड गोली चलायी। इस गोलीबारी में किसी के घायल होने की सूचना नहीं है।

किसान राजनैतिक दल के कार्यकर्त्ता तबतक गोली चलाते रहे जबतक पुलिस के वरीय पदाधिकारी एवं सशस्त्र दल पारथू गांव नहीं पहुंचे। सूत्रों ने बताया कि समझोता करने के लिए २० अक्टूबर की तिथि निर्धारित की गई है।

This incident indicates that negotiations start only after show of force to settle disputed cultuvable land. Instead of violence leading to negotiations for solution, the people must try to eliminate element of violence first and settle disputes amicably without depriving agriculture labours of their wages and agriculturists of the harvest.

27. The 73rd amendment of Constitution creating Panchayati Raj sys-
te[illegible] can generate atmosphere of peaceful settlement of disputes provided
[illegible] search solution earnestly. Presence of *asahanti* in villages/ panchyates
[illegible] negligence of development activities. People's purchasing power
[illegible]d in zones of *asahanti* and the poverty alleviation programmes
[illegible] affected. This explains the accentuation of the poverty alle-
[illegible] which of course can be reduced only by injecting income
[illegible]s to rural and urban people in shape of higher wages,

through gainful employment opportunities, self employment opportunities and productive investment of financial support given by the State and Centre.

Reference

1. Report of the Expert Group on Estimation of 'Proportion and Number of People: Planning Commission, Perspective Planning Division, Government of India, July 1993.
2. Annual Report of 1993-94, Department of Rural Development Government of India.
3. Annual Report of 1992-93, Department of Rural Development Government of India.
4. Annual Report of 1991-92, Department of Rural Development Government of Bihar.
5. Annual Report of 1993-94, Department of Rural Development Government of Bihar.
6. Annual Report of 1993-94, Department of Rural Development Government of Bihar.
7. Evaluation Report on Integrated Rural Development Programme: Planning Commission, Programme Evaluation Organisation, Government of India, May '85.
8. Basic Statistics Relating to Indian Economy-STATES-CMIE. September, 1993.
9. The Hindustan (Hindi), Patna daily, dt. 16.10.94.
10. District Estimates (Domestic Product) of Bihar 1990-91, Directorate of Statistics and Evaluation, Government of Bihar, December, 1993.
11. Peggy Antrpbus, Women and the Informal Sector "Development Journal of the Society for International Development, 1992-93.

Implementation of Poverty Alleviation Programmes

R.R. Prasad
S.K. Singh

The Plan strategy for fighting rural poverty has been confined to a direct attack on poverty through special employment programme like Integrated rural Development Programme (IRDP), Jawahar Rozagar Yojana (JRY), Employment Assurance Scheme (EAS), development programmes like Desert Development Programme (DDP) and Drought Prone Areas Programme (DPAP) and Land Reforms.

The large magnitude of investment for these rural development programmes requires that there should, be an appropriate delivery system at the level of district and below which should ensure that the funds are properly utilised to secure the intended objectives. It is, therefore, necessary to examine closely the delivery mechanism in order to identify areas of intervention and a secure optimum results.

With a view to studying the administrative and institutional arrangements for poverty alleviation programmes, a quick study was undertaken in the State of Bihar. Since the study of the delivery systems required critical examination of the administrative and institutional arrangements at the State, District, Block and Village levels, it was ensured that the systematic enquiries about the structure and processes of the delivery system be conducted at all these levels.

1. Objectives

(a) The specific objectives of the study were: to examine the existing administrative and institutional arrangements at various levels, and identify the bottlenecks and gaps, if any;

(b) to study the operational systems/ procedure followed for effective implementation of the poverty alleviation programmes *vis-a-vis* co-ordination across sectorial departments and DRDA;

(c) to analyses the process of planning and implementation of the programmes from the district to the Panchayat level;

(d) to identify the by-passed groups/areas under poverty alleviation programmes.

2. METHODOLOGY:

2.1 Study Area-Sample

The study was conducted in Ranchi district and in Angarha Block of this district in the State of Bihar. The sample for the study comprised beneficiaries of various poverty alleviation programmes and officials and non-officials engaged in the implementation of these programmes at Village, Block and District level. Information were also collected with Senior Officers at the State Level. For the purpose of PRA, interviews were held with the group of beneficiaries in each village Panchayats selected for the study.

2.2 Method of Data Collection

Primary data from the beneficiaries of the various poverty alleviation programmes were collected from four Panchayats, namely, Hasatu, Jaspur and Zonha. The villages selected for the study from each of the above Panchayats area Singari, Nagrabeda, Dublabeda, and Guridih.

For collecting primary data, besides use of field inventories, the techniques of key informant, group interview, case study and participatory Rural Appraisal were extensively used.

2.3 Programmes Studied

In this research, programmes like IRDP, TRYSEM, DWCRA, JRY, IJRY IAY, EAS Watershed Development Project, etc. were studied for understanding the administrative and institutional arrangements for implementation of these programmes.

3. Major Findings of the Study

3.1 Organisational Arrangements

(a) Although the State Level Co-ordination Committee (SLCC) has been constituted under the Chairmanship of the chief secretary, the meeting of the SLCC is not held regularly.

(b) The DRDA does not have staffing pattern as per the guidelines. The posts of APO, Accounts Officer and Accounts Assistant are vacant.

(c) At the block level, post of VKWs. are vacant, in the tribal sub-plan area of Ranchi, the posts of Joint BDO, 5 additional VLW and one additional VLW (women) have not been created (despite the provision for augmenting these posts in the IRDP Manual of 1991).

(d) There is a Block Level Consultative Committee (BLCC) and a Block Level Bankers' Committee (BLCC). There is poor co-ordination in the functioning of these committees.

(e) Awareness about the updated guidelines on IRDP as well as TRYSEM and DWCRA is poor among BDO and other officials of the block as well as district level officials. This has resulted in inadequate coverage of the targeted group of beneficiaries like SCs and STs, women, physically handicapped, ceilling surplus land assignees, green-card holders, and families who have adopted small family norms. The lack of awareness about the new provisions in the IRDP Manual has also resulted in non-implementation of the Group Life Insurance Scheme for IRDP beneficiaries, and not following the revised and simplified procedures for claiming benefits under the cattle insurance scheme.

(f) At the district level, an innovative approach, to decentralise and expedite the decision making process has been introduced viz. Abhiyan Uththan. Each officer of the rank of A.D.M/sub-divisional officer has been made in-charge of 2 blocks with full administrative powers to sanction projects selected in consultation with the people in the village itself. These officers are empowered to ensure proper selection, implementation and monitoring of schemes under various rural development programmes. This approach is expected to reduce the time gap between decision making process and execution of schemes.

(g) Another initiative that has been made at the district level is the constitution of special vigilance squad for monitoring and assessment of rural development programmes. It would also assess the problems of co-ordination across the sectoral departments.

(h) Under the Abhiyan Uththan, a Monitoring Committee has been constituted at the Sub-divisional level under the Chairmanship of the Sub-divisional officer (S.D.O.) which will monitor the implementation of rural development programmes in the Blocks falling under its juridiction.

3.2 Planning

(a) Perspective District Plan and the Annual Action Plan are being prepared for implementation of rural Development programmes at the district level.

(b) At the Block level, household surveys have been conducted to identify the families living below poverty line. List of identified beneficiaries belonging to different income groups and schemes to be given is available in printed form.

(c) The meeting of the Gram Sabha for selection of beneficiaries is held, but the final list of selected beneficiaries as reflected in the resolution of the Gram Sabha is not read out at the end of the meetings, thus leaving scope for manipulation at later stage.

3.3 Programme wise

I. IRDP

(a) The revised and updated format of VIKAS PATRIKA is neither available with the beneficiaries nor at the Block office.

(b) The schedule of inspection visits by the District and Block level officials for qualitative monitoring of the IRDP beneficiaries is not being adhered to.

(c) Credit camps for the selection of schemes for the targeted households, and documentation of loan application forms are not being organised.

(d) Generally there is no problem in sanctioning of loan applications by banks. Problems come only when the loan applications in a particular branch exceed the target fixed by the Bank. This reflects the poor co-ordination between the Block level officials, and the effectiveness of the BLCC and the BLBC.

(e) Banks are not using the discretion of giving 15% additional finance on special circumstances over and above the unit cost of the scheme.

(f) Monthly reports from Banks regarding number of IRDP applications received, approved and rejected are not being forwarded to the Block.

(g) The Bank officials are also not visiting the villages to attend to the problem of beneficiaries on non-working days. The system of cash disbursement by the Banks to the IRDP has also not been introduced.

(h) Unmarried women are being by-passed by the Block administration and the Banks. The unmarried women are not selected under IRDP. TRYSEM and DWCRA. Even if selected, the bank would not provide loans to them since it is defeated that after their marriage, they would move to other places and loan recovery would become difficult.

(i) There is a tendency among the Block level officials to avoid implementing rural development progrmmes in villages which are remote, inaccessible and have anti-social elements. Such neglect add to the problems of these areas, and emerge as by passed areas.

II TRYSEM

(i) There is considerable delay in release of stipends to the TRYSEM trainees.

(ii) Deviation from the guidelines was observed in terms of amount of stipend being paid to the TRYSEM trainees. Tool kit has not been provided to the trainees, payment of 50 per cent of the sale proceeds to the trainees for good produced during training is not being made. The District Level Committee for the follow-up of the TRYSEM scheme has not been constituted.

III. DWCRA

Most of the provisions under the programme has not been followed; to name a few: construction of Multipurpose Community Centres for DWCRA groups, registration of the group, formation of thrift and credit groups, constitution of advisory committees etc.

IV. JRY/IJRY/EAS/IAY

(a) Funds are not being made available in the beginning of the financial year, and hence, construction work to provide employment cannot be taken up during the period when the local labour has a lean season, and the climate is favourable.

(b) In the Block where intensified JRY has been introduced, the fund for regular JRY has not been made available. There is a confusion among the Block officials that the intensified JRY has been substituted with the regular JRY.

(c) The role of Panchayat has been eroded in the implementation of the intensified JRY as Panchayats have not been involved in the implementation of the intensified JRY.

(d) The allocation under social forestry component of the JRY is given to the Forest Department at the district level which implements the programes without co-ordination of the Block and consultation with the local people regarding choice of species.

(e) As regards EAS, the villagers seeking employment are not aware about the purpose, procedures and objectives of the scheme. Adequate efforts have not been made to apprise people about various provisions of the EAS.

(f) Houses under IAY were constructed within the unit cost with the active cooperation of the beneficiaries by going in for groups houses having a common wall, and working collectively for construction of group houses.

V. Watershed Development

(a) The watershed areas faced various problems such as severe soil erosion, low water holding capacity of the soils, poor fertility of soil. low cropping intensity, excessive biotic pressure on land, poor income levels etc.

(b) Allotment of funds for watershed projects was not done by the authorities, in full and it often got delayed. This resulted in late initiation of the planning and implementation of field level treatments in watersheds.

(c) Soil Conservation Department which is the major agency responsible for planning and implementation of the watershed programme, is doing excellent job both at conceptual and operational level. The field activities implemented by the department, therefore, demonstrated high degree of understanding.

(d) The inter-sectoral co-ordination was lacking due to which the expected synergy of effects of different field activities implemented by agriculture, soil conservation., forest, minor irrigation departments and the block agency could not be seen.

(e) Excellent example of people's participation in the creation and maintenance of water harvesting structure was observed. However, the participation in the watershed project as a whole was not forthcoming.

3.4 People's Participation

(a) No formal or informal or informal people's organisation exists to promote and protect the beneficiaries interest and welfare. The Panchayat Beneficiaries interest and welfare. The Panchayat Beneficiaries subcommittee (PBSE), Bank Area Baneficiaries Advisory Committee (BABC), and Block Level Beneficiaries Advisory Committee (BLBAC) have also not been constituted. However, a good network of voluntary organisations exist in the Block which are engaged in the upgradation and promotion of literacy among rural people.

(b) Peoples participation was adequately reflected in the construction of IAY houses. The beneficiaries could construct the houses under the unit cost by agreeing to go in for a common wall in the houses and by collectively working for construction of houses.

4. RECOMMENDATIONS

4.1 Organisational Arrangements

(a) The existing administrative and institutional arrangements at various level need to be properly toned up with emphasis on decentralisation in decision making powers.

(b) At the State level, a sub-committee of the SLCC may be constituted under Chairmanship of the Development Commissioner or the Secretary, Rural Development for taking decisions on urgent policy matters.

(c) The existing administrative structures at the District on Block level need to strengthened for coping with the ever increasing rural development programmes.

(d) The time taken in decision making process at the district, block and village levels in identification sanction and implementation of the schemes has been greatly reduced under the "Abhiyan Uththan" approach. This approach may be worth trying in other places.

(e) Gaps in the implementation process and observance of many procedures/guidelines emanate mainly due to lack of awareness among officials at various levels. With a view to making the officials/ non-officials at all levels fully aware about the procedures and guidelines for effective planning and implementation of rural development programmes, training should be made compulsory for them.

(f) Due to multiplicity of institutions for implementing rural development programmes which result in improper co-ordination and monitoring, it would be desirable to bring all the sectoral departments under the umbrella of Zila Parishad at the district level, and Panchayat Samiti at the Block level for facilitating better co-ordination and effective implementation.

4.2 Planning

(a) There is a need to lay special stress on the forward and backward linkages while planning for the income generating schemes for the rural poor.

(b) For ensuring effective participation of the rural people in all stages of planning and implementation of rural development programmes, people's participation should be made a built in component of the rural development programmes.

4.3 Programme-Based

(i) The unmarried adult women in rural areas should not be neglected under rural development programmes under the plea that after their marriage they would go away from the area. In fact, the skill acquired and income earned by them will go a long way in influencing their life as well as of future generations. The Banks should also have a positive attitude towards unmarried adult women, and they should not reject their loan applications. There is, however a need to work out the details of loan recovery process in case unmarried women move to other areas after their marriage.

(ii) Similarly, the remote and inaccessible areas infested with naxalite and extremists should be given to priority in development works instead of neglecting the area for further deterioration.

(iii) Under the JRY, the Panchayats have been made the executing agency. But the role of Panchayats has almost been eroded in the intensified JRY and EAS which has generated a feeling of neglect among the Panchayat functionaries. This approach also negates the idea of strengthening the grassroot level democratic institutions through their direct involvement in the implementation of rural development programmes. It is therefore felt that as far as possible, the Panchayat functionaries should also be involved in the implementation of intensified JRY and the EAS.

(iv) TRYSEM trainees should be first identified and selected as potential beneficiaries under IRDP, TRYSEM and DWCRA and subsequently given training under TRYSEM in the selected vocations. After acquiring necessary skills to manage the schemes, he/she should be assisted under IRDP for self-employment.

(vi) There should be group financing for the DWCRA groups instead of financing individual woman members under DWCRA.

(vii) Full and timely allocation of funds by the state level authorities is absolutely necessary to smoothen the process of timely initiation and completion of watershed projects.

(viii) Effective co-ordination between various implementing agencies is equally important for watershed projects which can be ensured through frequent meeting among the sectoral officers in the watershed project site itself. Their exposure to watershed activities will help them to observe the field activities in person and appreciate the problems thereunder.

Adequate publicity measures are needed to build up basic awareness about watershed projects among the people living in the watershed projects areas.

4.4 People's participation:

(i) With a view to encouraging people's participation in the rural development programmes, the committees of the beneficiaries at the Panchayat, Block and Bank level should be constituted.

(ii) Gram Sabha should be reactivated to ensure people's participation and involvement in rural development programmes.

•

Analysis of IRDP and Future Strategy

Rajlaxmi Rath

Since its inception in April 1978, the Integrated Rural Development Programme continues to be the major plank in the strategy for removal of poverty in the country. No doubt this programme has embedded in it the scope of general development of the rural areas but as a strategy the IRDP was designed with the primary objective of removal of poverty within a reasonable time frame, in a phased manner. It was designed to reach out to the people below the poverty line on an individual basis and help them get additional income, so as to enable them to cross the poverty line. Till the Fifty Five Year Plan it was found out that the benefits of planned development has been syphoned off by the more affluent sections, both in the rural and urban areas. Even programmes like SFDA, MFAL, DPAP, CADA which did have a target approach failed to make any significant dent in the situation of poverty alleviation of the general rural poor.

Objective and Strategy

The IRDP not only integrated all the above programmes, but also incorporated specific programmes for the sections of the rural poor who had no direct access to the process of planned development. To begin with any family whose annual income was below Rs. 3,500/- which was essential for the intake of 2,400 calories per head for a family of five, could become a beneficiary family. The Sixth Plan period (1981-86) raised the poverty line to Rs. 6,400/- per family annum. The poverty line has been raised upwards when ever necessary depending on the national price index.

The approach of IRDP is to provide the families living below the poverty line with assets and skills which will enable them to earn incremental income and become capable of crossing the poverty line. The families may include landless labourers, small and marginal farmers, rural artisans of all categories including scheduled castes and Scheduled Tribes, but will qualify only if they have income below the poverty line. In order to ensure that the SCs. STs and Women are not denied their due share a special emphasis that 30% of the total beneficiaries should be included from the above categories is insisted upon.

The focal point of the administrative set up for this purpose is the District Rural Development Agency (DRDA) in every district of the country. The DRDA under the chairmanship of the Collector plans, coordinates and implements the programmes. It has a full time project Officer, assisted by credit Plan Officer (drawn on deputation from the lead bank) and APO's in charge of agriculture, animal husbandry, sericulture, cooperation etc. The existing administration of the C.D/R.D. Department was also given the additional responsibility of implementing the IRDP at the village level. The BDO with his extension officers and the field level worker (VLW) was made a part of the delivery system of the IRDP. The indentified beneficiaries were asked to give their choice of a project/ asset and accordingly asked to fill up forms and complete the formalities. The application forms are then routed through the Block to the concerned branch of the Bank earmarked for the area. The bank after necessary scrutiny sanction the loan. A committee of officials namely the BDO, the block supervisor and the bank official as well as the beneficiary purchase the asset which is handed over to the beneficiary. The prescribed subsidy is released by the DRDA block in favour of the bank advancing the loan.

Achievements/Shortfalls

It one goes by the numerical results only, then IRDP targets were by and large achieved in the Sixth and Seventh Five Year Plan. This may give rise to a sense of satisfaction to the administrative machinery, but unfortunately the realities of the impact of this programme in eradication of poverty in the rural areas leaves much to be desired. The problem lies in the fact that whenever official reviews are conducted there is almost an obsession to achieve the quantitative targets of sanction and disbursement of loans and no attempt is made to find out if there has really been any quantitative improvement in the economic status of the beneficiaries as a result of this programme.

Several evaluation studies conducted by the RBI, Planning Commission, NABARD, NIRD and other organisations in different parts of the country have brought to light the following deficiencies.

1. Selection of Beneficiary

By and large IRDP has remained a government sponsored set of programmes, conceived, formulated as well as implemented solely by a parternalistic administration more as a set of welfare schemes rather than as economic or income-generating activities. The procedures adopted are rather mechanical and virtually nonparticipatory in nature. According to IRDP guidelines the target groups are to be identified after a baseline survey done by the VLWs. The selection is to be done through the Gram Sabha in the presence of all the villagers. The authenticity of the base line survey and the selection through Gram Sabha are often questionable. Tighter vigilance and effective supervision is necessary to ensure that the benefits accure to the most deserving among the rural poor.

2. Project Identification

The list of projects indentified is rather mechanical, unimaginative and tends to be uniform in all areas irrespective of wide variation in local conditions. In the identification of projects sometimes scant attention is paid to availability of local resourcees, need and capability of the beneficiaries, availability of support services and above all the avenues to fetch the additional income on a sustained basis. For example the incremental income that the milch animal project may fetch for the beneficiary has been calculated in the project design on a very high side. In reality such projects have not really helped large number of poor families to generate income enough to cross the poverty line. This is for the simple reason that in the selection and financing of this milch animal project sufficient attention is not paid to the breed of the animal, yield, price and availability of fodder, availability of veterinary services, processing facilities, market outlets price of the milk etc.

Programme

The experience with other live stock programme like goatery, piggery, poultry is no better. In addition to the infirmilities pointed out in the milchanimal projects it is found that the mortality rate in this category of livestock programme is quite high. The assistance given to beneficiaries under dairy, sheep-rearing, piggery, goat-rearing and other animal based schemes had marginal impact except for where the poor were already experienced in maintaining them. Besides a major reason for the failure of the livestock programme is low to nil availability of good quality animals particularly milch cows. Financing of bullock cart and camel cart have met with a similar fate. Here the beneficiaries were provided with monetary assistance without studying local condition or the need for such transport system. The result has been investments but no return.

Industries, Services and Business Sector (ISB)

There may be a great deal of scope here but what is required is greater effort on the part of the project and bank administration to devise locally suited schemes. This in turn calls for proper skills and training to be imparted to the beneficiaries to take up such projects in the I.S.B. Sector. Some positive outcome has been observed in cottage industry projects, weaving, artisan works with metal, leather based units, and shops. These schemes fared better and could bring reasonable income to the beneficiary. My own experience while visiting interior tribal areas of our neighbouring state of Orissa has been one of optimism Several households have been able to avail the bank loans and with the business of their tea stalls, grocery shops, cycle repairing units have been able to cross the poverty line, live a qualitatively better standard of living, after returning their bank loans and that too in a very short span of time. There seems to be more potential in this sector which has not been fully exploited in the anti-poverty programmes.

Minor irrigation sector

Loans to marginal and small farmers continue to be advanced under IRDP like the old SFDA and MFAL schemes. Inspite of the fact that some of the assets have been misutilised by the big farmers in the name of the poor farmers, yet studies have revealed that the performance in the minor irrigation sector has been good. The small and marginal farmers have benefited by the use of the assets like wells, borings, pumping sets financed to them to increase productivity of their land and earn higher returns from agriculture.

Crossing the Poverty line

No definite information is available as to the quantum of the incremental income that has accrued to the beneficiaries. There is no evaluation of the actual number of poor families who have actually crossed the poverty line and have continued to remain above the poverty line. Moreover wherever surveys have been conducted these are generally confined to calculating the gross income from the assets to the beneficiaries. The surveys generally do not deduct the annual repayment of bank loan from the additional income. The repayment of installments of loan is irregular. If proper decuction of the loan installments is done then, percentage of poor who are supposed to have crossed the poverty line will decline further considerably. Thus the picture is distorted and does not give a clear impression. In many cases the people below poverty line are regarded as having crossed the poverty line just by adding the loan component as their income.

As a plan of action the IRDP suffers from these major infirmities both at the level of conceptual frame work and at the level of implementation. Conceptually IRDP is supposed to integrate all the developmental activities. Very few persons, few families and equally few villages and districts were taken up or indentified for financial assistance in order to cross the poverty line. What is needed is a massive thrust in extending the programme to cover the major sections of people below the poverty line. Partial development of the poorest of the poor only is too modest an attempt at rural development. At the level of implementation too the same group of officials who look after law and order, family welfare, health, developmental schemes even natural calamites etc., and already overworked machinery cannot do the follow up of the IRDP schemes. These schemes ought to be attended to with utmost care and enthusiasm. What is required is specialised staff to carry out the tasks. There is hardly any expert available at the block level to help the beneficiary in the preparation of project report for filling loan application in the bank. As a result the banks do not find the projects suitable for financing. Hence the purpose of the IRDP schemes to assist the poor to cross the poverty line is lost.

Strategies to Improve IRDP Implementation

1. Co-ordination with other development programmes.

The IRDP programme cannot succeed unless it is properly co-ordinated with other development programmes. For example the most popular of all programmes the animal based programmes like dairy, piggery, goatery, sheep-rearing, cannot succeed unless they are supported by artificial insemination programme, fodder development, installation of milk processing centres, proper veterinary care etc. For what is extremely importants like animal husbandry, co-operative, agriculture etc. in order to sustain the scheme and help the beneficiary to generate income.

Similarly the Industries, Services, and Business Sector (ISB) needs proper co-ordination from the District Industries Centres for availability of imputs, marketing of products designing and upgradation of skills. Scope of cattle programme is limited for it is fraught with a lot of problems. But the scope under ISB is unlimited hence more stress should be given here. This will in the long run help in the diversification of the economy in the rural areas from agriculture to other sectors and be a major factor in assisting the rural poor cross the poverty line.

Excellent coordination of IRDP implementing agency and the bank is essential for the success of these anti-poverty programmes. Just by giving loans to these poorest of poor beneficiaries the problem cannot be solved.

Proper follow up action is required by the project officials. They should periodically check up the progress of the beneficiaries and help them solve any problems they face. Support mechanisms may be chalked out for recovery of the loans. Without proper motivation and 'help' by the Government Officers, bank staff and grass root politicians the beneficiaries unnecessarily become overburdened with loans and lands himself in a far more formulating worst position.

In formulating and identifying projects more attention should be paid to the suitability of the projects to local conditions. An ideal set of projects cannot be drawn and implemented for the entire country. The project should be such that it should suit the needs of the people of the area. The schemes should be flexible and innovative.

It is observed that influential sections of people may themselves get the benefits or pass it off to people who may be poor but not the 'poorest of the poor'. Utmost care must be taken at the selection point to choose carefully only the most deserving cases.

And above all marketing facilities of their products by the beneficiaries under the IRDP scheme should be provided for. There should be collection centres for milk so that the poor beneficiary does not have to bear the burden of selling his/her product. Products of cottage industries, handicrafts etc., can be collected from village to village by different units and sold at proper rates in towns/cities in the corporation showrooms. In this way the poor beneficiary gets motivated to produce more and more good and the real aim of IRDP to eradicate poverty can be achieved to a great extent.

People's Participation--Role of Voluntary Agencies

The IRDP shelf of schemes is hardly a set of doles, relief or welfare measures to the rural poor. It is essentially a people programme, which needs active participation of the people for successful implementation. The concerned officials may help the beneficiaries to draw the plan project, understand the scheme and solve any problem that arises during the implementation of the scheme and actively participate so that he can be successful in crossing the poverty line. The villagers can after the selection of the projects, be assisted and helped by organising themselves into village level group which may be formal or informal for the limited purpose of managing the project. Even prior to the actual selection of projects the villagers should be assisted to understand various choices and make selection as per their need. Thus people's participation would imply that the official agency should enlist the popular participation rather than implementing the schemes as a government sponsored programme. The objective here will be to create a flexible organisation at the local level, that can help the people in identifying their needs and relieve them through appropriate approach and support systems. The ideal strategy would envisage a coordinated effort of the government officials, bank and the people in alleviation of rural poverty.

The vital point therefore is as to who will organise the poor. A dedicated District Magistrate, BDO or VLW may achieve partial success but these examples are few and far between. The limitations these officials face are many. Their hands are full with the overall functioning of the district beginning from law and order to meeting natural calamities. This critical gap of organising the rural poor to make the best use of available potentials and resources for development can be best filled by the sector of Voluntary Agencies. The voluntary Agencies by their very nature are flexible informal and innovative in approach and some of these agencies have been engaged in various welfare and developmental activities. They can effectively plan the role of catalysts in the process of rural development. The Voluntary Agencies can not only create awareness among the rural people, but also secure their active participation in various self employment projects. In fact the VAS can be associated in all the process including, identification of beneficiaries, choice of assets, technical and managerial services, marketing and above all in bringing them together for their economic amelioration. This will create greater self-confidence and entrepreneurship among them. On their part the administration will have to play a positive role in encouraging the participation of Voluntary Agencies in the process of rural development.

References:

1. Government of India Ministry of R.D, Indian Awas Yojna (Manual) New Delhi,1992.
2. Government of India Ministry of R.D, IRDP and Programmes , (Manual) New Delhi. January, 1985.
3. Government of India Deptt. R.D, Ministry of Agriculture, IRDP and Allied Programmes of TRYSEM and DWCRA,(Manual) November,1986.
4. Jha A.K., "Third World Impact' Journal Transparent Weaknesses of Rural Development Programme in India, April, 1993.

•

Constraints in Rural Development: Brief Outline

Krishna Kumar Shrivastava

India has really progressed after independence. Its rural areas have also developed. However the achievement has not matched with the expectations aroused. The general condition of people's life prevailing around 1947 and their infrastructural requirements could not be sufficiently developed. This has contributed towards the existing hardship in rural areas. Comparatively urban areas have been developed. This has created difference in the standards of living among people of urban and rural areas. As a consequence thereof, people from rural areas are getting attracted towards urban areas, a phenomenon which has harmed the growth of both rural and urban regions.

Question is, how could such situation grow specially when Gandhiji wanted people to go to villages. Gandhiji had visualised village life to be happier and plentiful so as to attract people living in towns. This conception was also advanced by Sant Vinoba Bhave, Jaiprakash Narayan and other eminent thinkers. Keeping this perception in view, the community development programme had begun in the decade of fifties. Panchayats had been organised even earlier. These activities had promises of really developing the villages. But such thing could not occur.

In my view, the real hurdle occurred with the discontinuance of the community development programmes. Implementation of schemes under stage I and stage II programmes of community development had generated expectations among people. Sufficient Coordination was visible between the executors of these programmes and the gram punchayats. People's participation in the implementation of these schemes had generated new awakening in village life. A new zeal, a new commitment among local people became apparent because they exhibited concern for the proper implementation of the development schemes which they considered to be linked with the growth of their own villages. Despite such enthusiasm, the resultant effect needed more time to fructify. This was because of the in built centuries old foreign rule. This delay caused impatience in leadership both in centre as well as in states. Even bureaucracy became so perturbed that the community development programmes were discontinued at a stage when they had begun to exhibit the results of development. Thus the efforts of Shri S.K. Dey came to an end without any appreciable result. Administration, specially of development again started being centralised in the Central and State Governments. Delhi and Patna took over the control of development as a result of which the enthusiasm and environment of development which had been created through the implementation of C.D. programmes got extinguished. The process of development not only got stultified but took a new direction. The participation of punchayats started decreasing and people's participation almost became nil.

This directly affected the necessities of rural areas and its perception of development. Bureaucrats and politicians sitting in state capitals and centre began to formulate schemes. People of rural areas were denied the growth of their natural abilities and indigenous resources became neglected. Urban people started taking decision about the development of rural areas. Naturally rural people started getting alienated from the process of development which they began considering as imposed. This adversely affected the pace of development. In effect, schemes of human resources development like development of education, health and family welfare programmes suffered. It also adversely affected development of infrastructural growth like construction of roads, extension of transport and electricity. Agricultural growth and development of industrial activities also suffered in rural areas. Employment opportunities in rural areas could not increase. Rise in population could not be controlled. People in search of proper education, adequate health care, better living--facilities and personal security started migrating from villages to towns. No body specially those who get educated and acquire skill in any field now wants to stay in villages.

The seventy-third constitutional amendment has brought a ray of hope for involving people's participation. If the leadership of states and Centre fail to implement its provisions earnestly, the current difficult situation being faced by the country would further deteriorate. In such event celebration of Gandhi's memory would become perfunctory and our future generation would never forgive us.

Note:-- The original article is in Hindi. Its English translation has been done by Dr. H.K. Sinha, Executive Director of this Institute.

•

Hurdles to Rural Development

S.K. Sinha

WHAT IS RURAL DEVELOPMENT ?

Mahatma Gandhi

"If my dream is fulfilled and every one of the Seven Lakhs of villages, becomes a living republic in which no one is idle for want of work in which every one is usefully occupied and has nourishing food, well ventilated dwellings and sufficient Khadi for covering the body and in which all villagers know and observe the laws of hygiene and sanitation, such a state must have varied and increasing needs which it must supply unless it would stagnate".[1] The Gandhian concept of rural development was based on achieving self sufficiency of villages in which every one would have adequate food, shelter, clothing proper hygienic and sanitation facilities and every person willing to work is provided gainful employment.

The 1948 Cambridge conference of Community Development defined Rural Development as "a movement to promote better living for the whole community with the active participation and if possible on the initiative of the community but if this initiative is not forthcoming by the use of techniques for arousing and stimulating it in order to secure its active and enthusiastic response to the movement".[2]

World Bank

'Rural Development is a strategy designed to improve the economic and social life of a specific group of people —the rural poor. It involves extending the benefits of development to the poorest among those who seek a livelihood in rural areas. The group includes the small scale farmers, tenants and the landless. The central concept of rural development is of a process through which rural poverty is alleviated by sustained increases in the productivity and incomes of low income rural workers and households. The emphasis is on raising output and income rather than simply distributing current income and existing assets. Although the latter may be desirable or even essential than over all rural development strategy which Links production with distributive or equality objectives. Operationally this concept of rural development requires that target groups specified among the rural poor for whom specific measures to raise production and income can be designed and in whose case the resulting flow of benefits direct and indirect is both identifiable and potentially measurable. The notion of target groups lies at the root of the definition of rural development as a separate and distinct component of general development as a separate and distinct component of general development strategy. It provides that necessary focus on groups of the rural population in terms of whose well being policy actions and programme can be designed and evaluated. The operational goals of rural development exceed beyond any particular sector. They include improved productivity and higher incomes for the target groups as well as minimum acceptable levels of food, shelter, education and health service. Fulfillment of these objectives call for an expansion of goods and services available to the rural poor and institutions and polices that will enable them to benefit fully from the whole range of economic and social services".[3]

Rural Development has of necessity to be broad based and oriented towards improving the economic and social life of the rural poor. Hence the rural-development efforts must include a mix of projects and programmes aimed at not only increasing the productivity, production and income levels of the rural poor but also improving health and education, expanding transport and communication and developing housing and wide variety of other rural services.

Objectives of Rural Development

The objectives of Rural Development in the Indian context can be summarised as under:

(i) To promote a healthy outlook and right type of attitude among the village men, women, youth and children for total transformation of the rural community and to develop a spirit of development mindeness rather than facility mindedness.

(ii) To maximise agricultural production by effective and efficient utilisation of land and water resources.

(iii) To effectively implement the land reforms by distribution of surplus lands utilisation of cultivable waste lands backed by adequate provision of agricultural inputs to the allottees.

(iv) To promote rural industrialisation particularly agro based industries.

(v) To create maximum gainful employment opportunities in the rural areas by diversification of the occupational structure at the village level.

(vi) To ensure that the benefits of development accrues more and more to the rural poor direct without any grabing by middlemen.

(vii) To have maximum participation and involvement of the prospective beneficiaries in the identification, preparation and implementation of the rural development programmes.

(viii) To ensure supply of adequate and timely credit for production and development purposes to the rural poor.

(ix) To provide basic infrastructural facilities rural roads, rural transport, rural electrification etc.,

(x) To contain population growth by providing requisite educational and health facilities, family planning facilities particularly for the rural poor.

Rural Development In India

Since the advent of planning in 1951 a number of rural development programme have been implemented. Some of them were:

(1) Community Development Programme (CDP) 1952

(2) Intensive Agricultural Development Programme (IADP) 1960-61

(3) Intensive Agricultural Areas Programme (IAAP) 1962

(4) Rural Industries Project (RIP) 1962-63

(5) Rural works and Manpower Programme (RWM) 1964

(6) High Yielding Varieties Programme (HIPV) 1966

(7) Tribal Area Development Programme (TADP)

(8) Small Farmers Development Agency (SFDA) 1971-72

(9) Marginal Farmers and Agricultural Labourer Development Agency (MFAL) 1971

(10) Crash scheme for Rural Employment (CSRE) 1971-74

(11) Land Army Organisation of Karnataka (LAO) 1971

(12) Pilot Intensive Rural Employment Project (PIREP) 1972

(13) Employment Guarantee Scheme Maharashtra (EGS) 1972

(14) Drought Prone Areas Programme (DPAP) 1973

(15) Command Area Development Programme (CADP) 1974

(16) Twenty Point Economic Programme 1975

(17) Minimum Needs Programme (MNP) 1975

(18) Hill Area Development Programme (HADP) 1974-75
(19) Food for Work Programme (FFWP) 1977
(20) Integrated Tribal Development Programme (ITDP) 1976-77
(21) Integrated Rural Development Programme (IRDP)
(22) Training of Rural Youth for self Employment (Trysem) 1979
(23) National Rural Employment Programme (NREP) 1980
(24) Rural Landless Employment Guarantee Programme (RLEGP) 1983
(25) Development of Women and Children Rural Area (DWCRA) 1982-83
(26) Jawahar Rojgar Yojna (JRY) 1989
(27) Employment Assurance Scheme (EAS) 1993

Despite a plethora of rural development programme implemented in the last 40 years as enumerated above the rural scene in India has not materially changed as may be observed from the fallowing facts:

(i) The rural population has increased from 299 million in 1951 to 629 million in 1991. Birth rate is still 29.5 per thousand.
(ii) According to the latest data available 33.4 per cent of the people in rural areas are still poor.
(iii) Literacy rate in rural areas hovers around 44 per cent, 70 per cent of rural women are illiterate.
(iv) More than 40 per cent of our villages are not served by surface roads.
(v) Only 2.46 per cent of the population in rural areas is covered with sanitation facilities.
(vi) About 1.53 lakh out of 5.76 lakh villages are partially covered by drinking water facilities.
(vii) The total backlog of housing for the country is estimated at 31 million of which 20.6 million are in the rural areas.
(viii) The top 39 percent own 80 percent and lowest 30 per cent own only two per cent of the assets in rural areas.
(ix) More than 70 per cent of the farmers are small and marginal having less than 2 hectors of land and own only 24 per cent of the cultivated area.
(x) Agriculture which is the main occupation in rural areas is overloaded and productivity per acre is very low as compared to other countries. Only 30 per cent of our cultivable land is provided with irrigation facilities.
(xi) Modern health care systems are beyond the reach of the most rural people.
(xii) Infrastructural inadequacies still exit with lack of proper commu-

nication, transport, electrification etc.

(xiii) The occupational structure in the rural areas has not been diversified and rural industries are yet to be developed.

(xiv) Base level organisations like co-operatives and Panchayats are not well managed and developed.

(xv) Voluntary agencies in the field of rural development are few and far between and the rural poor are not organised.

(xvi) The benefits of rural development have not accrued to the really poor and deserving people to the desired level.

(xvii) The villages are yet to become worth living and the flight of rural people to urban areas continues unabate. This is mainly due to lack of employment opportunities in rural areas and rural urban wage differentials apart from worsening law and order situation.

HURDLES TO RURAL DEVELOPMENT

(i) Rising Rural Population:

The rural population of India is increasing from year to year. It increased from 299 million in 1951 to 629 million in 1991.

In retrospect all rural development efforts are being neutralised by the growing rural population. There is need to have a movement for population control otherwise all our schemes of rural development will have little or limited success. No rural development is possible without population control and unless there is rural development, population control in the rural areas cannot be made effective. Hence they have to go together. Unfortunately we have not been able to take hard and have effective decision for population control and our family planning efforts have failed to go beyond making a lot of propaganda. Rigorous incentives and disincentives are required to be provided so that a consciousness is around to limit the size of the family. There is no integration of rural development programme with family planning programme in rural areas.

(ii) Defective Implemention of Land Reforms

Land is the most important source of living for majority of the people in rural areas. Ownership of Land howsoever small in size provides a social-economic status and dignity for a rural family. The Land Reform measure have not been enforced effectively as may be seen from the following facts:-

1. Voluntary organisation in Rural Indian society of Agricultural Economics Senior Series XII. page 16.
2. Community and their Development by T.R. Bawen-Oxford University Press London. page-1.
3. Assault on world poverty problems of Rural Development, World Bank Publication. page 3.

(a) The Land which has been declared surplus has not been distributed or even taken possession of. The cumulative progress in implementing the land ceiling laws during the successive plan periods was as under:-

Pre-revised and Revised Ceiling laws (Figures in million acres)

	As on 31.8.80	As on 31.3.85	As on 31.3.90	As on 31.3.93
Area declared surplus	69.13	72.07	72.25	73.52
Areas taken possession	48.50	56.98	62.12	64.15
Area distributed	35.58	42.64	46.47	50.42

(b) The Land received under Bhoodan movement but not yet distributed was about 2.9 million acres.

(c) There is an area of about 40 million acres of cultivable wasteland which has not been properly utilised and developed.

(d) There are several cases of illegal land grabs by dominant person in the village for which no records are available.

Although in the Seventh Five Year Plan itself it was emphasised that Land Reforms would form an intrinsic part of the anti-poverty strategy and should be taken up as a conjuctive activity alongwith other rural development programme, the progress made in the direction of land reforms does not appear to be very encouraging. The reasons for the slow implementation of land reforms are defective land legislation, inadequate administrative machinery, prolonged litigation, unupdating of land records, lack of political will on the part of the states. The Land reforms have to be rigorously enforced and the various operational bottlenecks removed once for all so that the benefits of land reforms may accrue to the maximum number of landless.

(iii) Illiteracy

About 55 per cent of the rural people are illiterate and illiteracy among rural females is still higher. Illiteracy is a great stumbling block for the socio-economic development of the rural poor who are mostly fatalists and accept poverty as a way of life. The poor illiterates cannot assert themselves and often reconcile to their fate. Thus lack of human capital in the rural areas is one of the greatest hindrances in the way of rural development. The main reason for the failure of family planning programme is the rampant illiteracy among rural women. Eradication of illiteracy among the rural people both by formal and informal methods of education is a must if we want to eradicate poverty. Literacy should therefore be made an integral component of the rural development programme.

(iv) Lack of Effective Voluntary Agencies

The Seventh Five Year Plan formulated in 1985 envisaged an operational arrangement for promotion of voluntary efforts primariy in the field of rural development. Voluntary organisations were given the freedom to plan their own schemes and follow a methodology they think best to tackle poverty in villages in which they work. Stress was laid on professionalism of voluntary services. The voluntary organisations were urged to moblise locally available human and financial resources, identify the poor farmers, rural artisans, SC, and STs, agricultural workers and bonded labourers, upgrade their skills and give them the tools to attain economic self-reliance. The approach to the Seventh five Year Plan (1985-90) rightly observed. "In the ultimate analysis the objective of removal of poverty can be fulfilled in the measures in which the poor themselves become conscious, improve their education and capabilities and become organised and assert themselves." The role of voluntary agencies has further become important in the changed context of implementing the rural development programme through Panchayati Raj Institutions.

(v) Lack of People's Participation:

The Rural Development Programme by and large have been government sponsored with the result that they virtually become programmes of the Government and not of the people. The participation of the people in the programmes meant for their development is absolutely necessary if the programmes have to be made realistic and need-based.

The rural beneficiaries at present are not organised with the result that they are not the spokesmen of their own problems and others who are not concerned with the local problems manage the show.

Recently after the 73rd amendment of the Indian Constitution in April 1993 the Panchayti Raj Institutions have been given the responsibility of implementing the rural development programmes. The Panchayati Raj Institutions can serve the interests of the poor only if a majority of the seats and posts of Presidents and Chairman at all the three tiers are reserved for agricultural Labour, small and marginal farmers and artisans, Scheduled Castes and Scheduled Tribes as recommended by the parliamentary Committee on Agriculture (J. Chokka Rao Committee).

For making peoples participation effective in the implementation of rural development programmes it is necessary to organise the poor. As suggested by the committee to Review the Administrative Arrangement for Rural Development and Poverty Alleviation Programmes (CAARD) the objectives of any programme for the organisation of the poor should inter-alia be:

(a) to increase the level of awareness of the target groups in regard to the programme content and facilities provided therein under the programmes.
(b) To encourage their participation in planning and implementation of these programmes.
(c) To increase their bargaining power through group action
(d) To promote co-operative and group action among beneficiaries.
(e) To establish a feed back mechanism and appropriate forum where a constant dialogue could take place between Government functionary groups at village level and
(f) To make the beneficiary groups self-reliant that is the group/individual increasingly learns to do for themselves/ himself what was done for them/him previously by others.

Unless the poor are organised at the village level, they cannot enforce effective implementation of the rural development programmes. Voluntary agencies can play an important role in organising the rural poor. The voluntary agencies can mobilise rural people and organise them by making them aware of their duties and responsibilities and advantages of the rural development programmes. Continuous flow of relevant information for the rural poor can be possible only when they are organised.

(vi) Lack of Commitment on the Part of the Local Level Bureaucracy

As observed by the Parliamentary Committee on Agriculture the most important factor for the tardy performance of IRDP is the lack of commitment and dedication on the part of the officials connected with identification, formulation, appraisal, monitoring and evaluation of the various rural development schemes. At the same time dedicated officers are also subject to harassment and the end result is that the finance for implementing the schemes instead get sidelined. The local level development functionaries must be responsive to the needs of the rural people and help them by providing proper guidance into proper selection of development projects.

(vii) Planning at Microlevel

A major weakness of the rural development programme lies in the planning process presently followed. The DRDAS draw the annual plans. This had more or less degenerated into an arithmetical exercise tailoring the programme to the amount of capital subsidy proposed to be made available. The plan should be prepared taking into account the felt needs of a particular area in due consultation with the local people.

It has been observed that no efforts are made to examine the feasibility of the activities to be undertaken in a block with reference to the forward and backward linkages available. There is sometimes an over-emphasis on certain activities and other equality important activities are neglected Preference of identified beneficiaries are not taken into consideration and programme are not structured with reference to the potential for different activities to be undertaken in the area.

(viii) Delayed, Untimely and Sometimes Inadequate Availability of Credit.

There are a number of credit based poverty alleviation programme to enable the rural poor emerge out of their poverty by undertaking productive schemes for generation of additional income. It has been observed that in many cases the credit disbursed are not adequate and prompt. Delayed, inadequate and untimely credit is mainly responsible for the large scale misutilisation and default of credit.

"The factors which constraint the capacity of the poor to borrow from organised credit Institutions are lack of skill, unawareness of economic opportunities and of markets, what they are capable of producing and their inability to over come bureau credit requirements".

(Dr. C. Rangarajan, Governor, RBI)

Provision of adequate and timely availability of credit to the identified beneficiaries for selected schemes of development must be ensured.

(ix) Recovery of Dues

The one big problem affecting the implementation of integrated rural development programme is the unsatisfactory pace of recovery of the IRDP Loans. The recovery performance of banks in respect of IRDP loans during the last four years ending 1992 was as under:

(Rs. in Crore)

Year ended June	Demand	Recovery	Overdues	% of recovery to demand
1989	9129	356	554	39.1
1990	1069	330	739	30.8
1991	1272	526	746	4103
1992	1439	452	987	31.8

While the reasons for heavy incidence of overdues may be due to incorrect identification of beneficiaries and actives, poor quality of lendings, defective loan appraisal, inadequate availability of proper infrastructure, inadequate incremental income of the beneficiary etc., the co-operation and support of the Government agencies in recovery efforts of banks is often more than lacking.

Remedies

(1) Participation and involvement of the people in the identification, preparation and implementation of the schemes meant for their development is very important. The beneficiaries should be organised into functional groups so that they by themselves manage the schemes properly without reliance on outside agencies.

(2) Under the 73rd constitutional amendment 1993, Panchayats have been assigned the task of rural development. The Panchayati Raj Institutions, however, will serve the purpose and interests of the poor only if a majority of seats and posts of Presidents and Chairman at all the three tiers are reserved for agricultural labour, small and marginal farmers and artisans.

(3) It is also necessary to change the existing co-operataive Laws to bring the village co-operatives within the control of small and marginal farmers, agricultural labourers and other deprived categories. Political will is necessary for such a basic reorientation of the rural development programme.

(4) Infrastructural facilities both quantitatively and qualitatively need to be improved. Rural Roads, Irrigation facilities, Rural electrification etc., should be given priority in any programes of rural development.

(5) Effective implementation of the land reforms covering ownership rights,. enforcement of land ceiling, distribution of surplus land and its development is a must to augment the usefulness or rural development programmes. The legal loopholes must be plugged and the land reform laws should be made more rigorous so as to secure a large and resource for the rural poor.

(6) Containment of population growth should be an important part of the rural development programmes and family planning incentives must be provided in appropriate measure to the beneficiaries of the rural development schemes. The family planning programmes and the rural development programme should be integrated and go together.

(7) Voluntary agencies should be encouraged to take up rural development programme by introducing a village adoption scheme on a cluster basis for all-round integrated rural development. The

work of monitoring follow up and training should be entrusted to voluntary agencies.

(8) Agro-based rural and cottage industries should be promoted on a more extensive scale by adopting a comprehensive plan of rural industrialisation.

(9) Effective penal measures would be necessary to combat the evils of leakages of funds and consequent corruption presently prevailing in administration of rural development programmes.

(10) Monitoring cells at the block, district and state levels should be promoted and activised to ensure regular and effective supervision over the rural development programmes. The voluntary agencies may be involved in this task.

(11) Special attention should be paid to recovery of IRDP Loans so that the flow of credit under IRDP could be maintained smoothly. All possible assistance should be given to the banks by the District and Block authorities to facilitate this task. The Government should refrain from adopting populist measures like loan melas, loan postponement of recoveries etc.

(12) The last but the least important strategy should be to launch a time bound formal and informal educational programme for the illiterate rural beneficiaries as has been done in the World Bank assisted projects in African countries.

•

What Ails our development Efforts?

A case for a Shift in Strategy

Gopinath T. Menon

Till a few years back "Development" was seen as the key to all humanity's problems— whether it was poverty, unemployment, illiteracy or hunger. We can even recall statements which placed development as the best contraceptive to tackle the problem of population growth. There is no doubt that development is indeed the only long term solution to all the sufferings that humanity face today. Unfortunately the term development is so wide and all comprehensive that it means many things to many people. Defining development in itself is a major challenge and therefore planning for development becomes equally challenging and complex. Many models of development planning have evolved over the years and in India, we too have been experimenting with various concepts since independence. While very impressive advances have been made in many fronts we are still far away from gaining salvation from the very things that we have been fighting against viz. poverty, hunger, malnutrition death, illiteracy and the unbridled population growth. Huge investments have gone into agriculture, industry, infrastructural development and education. And yet for almost half of our population life has not only not improved but may have even become worse. The frustration and agony is much worse today than it was decades ago.

What went wrong? Perhaps it is foolish tomake and attempt to analyse the reasons for failure in a short article of this kind. But it definitely is worth to reflect on our achievements and failures so that we learn important lessons for the future. It is with this spirit that I attempt an analysis of the situation.

Development Vs Sustainable Development

First of all let us try to define 'development,' it is only a proper understanding of this that will enable us to make a headway. And while doing so it is extremely important that we make the distinction between development and sustainable development. In the kind of development processes that we have pursued the poor and the marginalised as well as all those living below the poverty line were our 'targets' for development. Thus in the social sector it became the responsibility of the state and the well to do communities to see that the above groups are 'developed' and provided for. Thus government took on the role of the 'PROVIDER' making services available to the 'target groups' with the noble objective of raising the standard of living of the 'target group'. We also created a massive infrastructure that practically reached out to every village of the country under the Community Development Programme launched in the early sixties. Similarly an elaborate pyramidal structure reaching right up to every community was created for providing primary health care for our people. Even in the case of education the state took on the role of the provider, especially in the primary education sector, with more and more states nationalising this sector. Similar efforts have been made by the government practically in every sector be it water, child development or social forestry. The results too have been far reaching. The globally praised green revolution which has given the country millions of tons of food as a buffer stock, the large army of highly qualified and skilled professionals, health care facilities with super specialities that could compete with anywhere in the world, a strong and vibrant industrial and commercial sector which is well posed to take on the onslaught of multinationals etc. are a few of the many that the country can be truly proud of.

Yet the irony remains. Poverty among plenty; rates of illiteracy (every fourth illiterate in the world is an Indian) that shames all the wonderful universities and educational institutions that we have created; a wholly unacceptable rate of infant and child mortality that defies the strides we have made in the medical and health care sector and a population growth rate that still threatens our future. We could go on listing this paradoxical situation which should shock us from our slumber. How can we remain silent when we loose about 10,000 under five year olds every day for no fault of theirs but for our failures? Why should a woman die almost every four minutes in the process of giving birth to a new life into this world? Why should diarrhoea and acute respiratory infections continue to take such a heavy toll of our children when they could easily be handled at the community level? How do we continue to allow about a 40% of our children still to remain outside any kind of an educational process when our Constitution aims at guaranteeing free elementary education to every child till it completes 14 years? Why do women and girl children continue to be discriminated against when we have guaranteed them equal status and equal opportunities in shaping their lives and living?.

The above context forms the backdrop of our community development on the role of the state as a development agency where the people for, whom the services are meant remain as target groups or mere 'beneficiaries', while most of our community development documents have compulsorily highlighted community participaton as the key process for most of our developmental activities, we have some how failed in translating this into a reality. The 'beneficiaries' have remained as beneficiaries and we have not succeeded in making them partners with the government in executing the programmes for their development. This, I believe, to be the single most important factor for our failure to make any significant dent on the core issues that continue to plague our society. The great development strides that we have made remain beyond the reach of the large segment of our communities.

The old Chinese saying "Give a man a fish he lives for a day; teach him how to fish he lives for a lifetime" is indeed a very critical lesson in development planning. For sustainable development to take place the 'target groups' or 'beneficiaries' need to be brought to the centre stage where decisions regarding their lives are made by them and there is an ownership of programme activities by them. Community organisation for group action then becomes central to execution of any development programme. Thus true development should focus on helping the members of the community to come together for identification of their common problems and; (felt) needs, planning out strategies/activities to tackle them, implementing and monitoring the activities that they had planned all with or without outside support. This process of community organisation and group action leads to capacity and confidence building which in turn leads to a self reliant approach to the development agencies play the role of catalysts facilitating the above process and helping people to hold themselves. Thus for sustainable development people cannot be targets or beneficiaries but should take the centre stage in the planning and execution of programmes. And we need to realize that there is no shortcut to this process.

Once the government and many of the development agencies could get over the mind set that they are the 'providers' and accept that it is only the so called beneficiaries who are really capable of changing their destiny it will be easy for us to see that the money and other resources that we have with us are only tools or mens that would help us in reaching out to the communities for their organisation and action for development. If this approach is accepted, it then calls for a major shift in our strategy for programme/service delivery.

From Targets and Outputs to Building People

Today a large number of programmes under various departments are being implemented at the village level with a number of sectorial functionaries shouldering the responsibilities. The DRDAs implement the Integrated Rural Development Programme (IRDP) the Development of Women and Children in Rural Areas (DWCRA) the Assured Employment Programme as well as the Indira Awaas Yojana in addition to many others. The Health Sector besides having its primary health care programme also implements programme in immunisation, diarrhoea control, leprosy, malaria and a host of other programmes. The Social Welfare Department runs the Integrated Child Development Scheme (ICDS) through a network of Anganwadi centres. The Education department has its own primary schools in practically every village. Thus a number of functionaries are reaching out to the village community with various services under each umbrella. They hardly meet together to discuss common problems and plan jointly for taking up activities together and work independently. There is very little attempt made at coordination and convergence at all the different levels thus failing to capitalise on the resources available to supplement and complement each other.

In any given village/panchayat the following functionaries are generally available:

1. Village level worker	2. Gram sevak
3. Multi Purpose Health worker (male)	4. Multipurpose health worker (female)
5. Trained Village Dai	6. Primary school teachers
7. Anganwadi worker and helper	8. Panchayat member

This is supported by a supervisory staff from the different departments.

Unfortunately these workers have not been provided with a clear understanding of their role as development worker. The major focus in their training activity has been to help the workers acquire basic skills in the delivery of services that they are required to provide. The entire process of a clear appreciation for the need for community mobilisation and organisation for group action in their own area of work is missed out. Unless the functionaries are made to realise that community's involvement in the programme activities through a well planned out process is central to their success. We will be falling short of our targets. This calls for a complete reorientation of our training activities in all the programmes where the focus should be to help the trainees acquire skills in community organisation for their active participation and ownership of all activities—be it health, education, agriculture, income generation or any other.

Instead of setting only targets/outputs under each programme we need to also set clear cut goals in the area of community organisation. In other words development needs to be measured in terms of the community participation in the different levels of programme implementation as well as the extent of their ownership of the programme. Once the targets and goals get systematically monitored the functionaries too will starts understanding the priority for community education and organisation which in the long run will make their work easy and enjoyable.

A Holistic Approach to Programme Planning and Implementation

For effective community mobilisation and organisation it is very important that all the functionaries working with the community combine together and work as a term. Once common goals and targets for community mobilisation and organisation is set up and an activity plan with time schedule is worked out for achieving the targets and goals the functionaries will gain a better appreciation of their role with the community as well as the suctorial services that they provide. With a team approach to their work each functionary will be able to complement the other and together their combined output will be far greater. Once the community too understands their role, problems start getting resolved themselves and the synergic effect will be an accelerated pace of achieving sectorial as well as overall development goals on a sustainable basis.

19

Failure of Motivation and Human Progress:

The India-Bihar case

Abhas Chatterjee

When a topic like 'Causes of failure of rural development in Bihar 'Factors behind agrarian backwardness of Bihar' or 'What retards Bihar's agricultural growth' is chosen as the subject of discussion in a seminar or workshop, one generally tends to get psychologically trapped in a three-fold error of perception.

Bihar's Rural under-development is a fact:

(1) The 'failure' backwardness or retardation is pecullar of Bihar whereas the rest of India is performing very satisfactorily.

(2) That the failure of Bihar is, at least primarily in the field of rural development as opposed to urban development or other fields of activity such as industrial, social or intellectual development.

(3) One tends to mistake what essentially are symptoms of a larger malady as organisms causing the sectorial disorder of rural under-development.

One therefore frequently comes across articles which start with a convincing array of facts and figures to prove that by every reasonable yardstick of rural development. Bihar has been the poorest performer in India, but relapse thereafter into an analysis of causes which is no more than a statement of disjointed generalities without any logical connection or statistical support.

A typical paper on the causes of the rural stagnation would, for example, point out that the percapita rural income of Bihar (in 1980-81) at Rs. 450/- was the lowest of all major Indian States (corresponding all-India average. Rs. 710), the growth rate of agricultural production (1962-65 to

1970-73) in Bihar was a paltry 0.54% (corresponding all-India average, 1.97%) rising in the subsequent decade (1970-73 to 1980-83) only to 0.60% (corresponding all India average 2.21%) and the average yield of rice per hectare (1982-83) in Bihar was only 816 kg (all India average 1230 kg) and wheat 1324 kg (all India average 1836 kg).

Such an article may also inform us that in the early years of post British rule, Bihar was not such a laggard. During 1952-53 to 1964-65 growth rate of agricultural production in Bihar at 2.97% was nearly equal to the national average (3.01%), but she fell behind with time. The progressive loss of her momentum is reflect in the fact that till 1977-78 Bihar had 57.8% of her rural population below poverty line (all India average 51.2%) which was lower than the figures of West Bengal, Maharashtra, Madhya Pradesh, Tripura, Orissa and Meghalaya, but within the next six years, she became the most poverty-afflicted State in India. In 1983-84, Bihar showed 51.4% of her rural population below poverty line which was the highest in the country (all India average 40.4%).

Common Misperceptions Regarding Causes

However, when the same article would proceed to identify the causes of this tragedy of Bihar, it would almost invariably end up with such superficiality as enumeration of phenomena like non availability of modern inputs and extension services, effect of permanent settlement and Zamindari system, chronic shortage of electricity, under utilization of irrigation potential, failure of co-operative movement, notorious inefficiency and corruption of the State Government, poor implementation of laws, poor infrastructure development and so on. Marxist writers in particular would feel satisfied by placing all the blame on the door of their betenoire: 'semi-feudal agrarian structure', dominant class-interest inimical to rapid growth, 'exploitative agrarian structure hampering diffusion of technology', redtapism and bureaucratic delay', 'continued legacy of zamindari system' leading to consolidation of feudal forces', 'farmers engrossed in feudal ethos and exploitation', 'elite domination', and so on and so forth.

Authors of such articles do not bother to ask how the 'legacy of feudal agrarian structure' can explain poor generation of electricity, or the State's failure to provide inputs in time, or the low availability of institutional credit, or 'poor water-management by the State apparatus'. They do not try to answer how if Zamindari system was at the root of Bihar's rural sickness, she managed to compare favorably with other Indian states till the end of the 150 years of prevalence of that system and started lagging behind only after she abolished the system, the first to do so in the country. They do not see the obvious contradiction between their thesis that there was 'complete stagnation in agricultural production in Bihar during the British period" with their own statistical evidence that Bihar's current slump did not start until a dozen years after the British left the country. [2] They avoid answering the obvious questions why other states under zamindari system, like Bengal and (of late, even) Orissa have overtaken Bihar. Faced with a complete failure of their hypothesis to explain many supposed causes of Bihar's lassitude, these authors often end up simply bewailing, "unfortunately, this did not happen in Bihar". Looking at Bihar's rural under-development in isolation, they overlook her equally dismal record in other areas of human activity and the possible connection between these failures.

Such articles also conveniently by-pass the vital question whether India's performance as a whole Bihar or no Bihar on the fronts of rural and other development activities since the British transferred power to Indian hands half a century ago can be considered a success-story, a record of rapid growth or an impressive march forward.

The correct perspective

Any, realistic analysis of rural Bihar's woeful performance thus requires an outset recognition of three basic facts:

(a) Bihar's failure on the rural development front is only a part of her larger failure on every other front viz; industrial, social, moral, educational and infrastructural,

(b) The latter in turn is a part, albeit more prominent, of a still larger failure of India as a whole, and

(c) What appears through the narrow aperture of suctorial analysis to be 'causes' of failure on rural front are indeed reflections or indexes of the larger failure.

Undeniably, terms like failure, slow, retarded etc. are all relative terms. Bihar's performance in rural development is poor in relation to other states or regions of India, just as India's performance is poor in relation to other countries relevant for the purpose of comparison. At the same time, no matter what yardsticks one chooses, Bihar would be found to have an equality miserable record in other fields of human progress. To get a right prospective, therefore, one must look at all these relativities simultaneously.

India Compared to other Countries

The most relevant comparison of India's performance will be with other large countries of South east or South East Asia which have had some 40/

2. A typical Marxist explanation for this phenomenon is that following abolition of zamindari, the 'feudal forces, were shellshocked in the '50s and so better rural growth was achieved in the' 60s, these forces re-grouped and so the slump ensued. How wonderfully simple!

50 years of relatively peaceful time to shape their societies and economies by now, viz. China, Pakistan, Indonesia, Sri Lanka, Malaysia, Thailand and South Korea. Some indicators of the relative economic development of these countries are therefore given in Table 1. It would be evident from the Table that India stands at the very bottom of the list in terms of per capita GNP, per capita merchandize exports and per hectare consumption of fertiliser. Except for Pakistan she also the lowest life expectancy at birth and adult literacy whereas in the negative indicators of 'infant mortality rate and total fertility of rate, she has the highest figure, again with the lone exception of Pakistan. India has the lowest per capita energy consumption except for Sri Lanka and Pakistan except for Indonesia she also carries the most strenuous burden of repaying external debts every year. The bottom line of the Table also shows that India is just above the average of the poorest 41 countries of the world (which the World Bank groups as low income countries), in terms of per capita GNP, whereas, in all other indicators, she is far below the average even in this group.

Table 1 : Basic Development Indicators (Country-wise)

Country GNP	Per capita merchandise ($)	Per capita exports ($)	Per capita energy consumption oil equi. ment kg	Per hect. ferti. consumption kg.	Adult literacy %	Total external debt service as % of exports	Life exptancy at birth Years	Total fertiliy rate	Mortality rate (per)0 live birth)
	1989	1989	1989	1987-88	1985	1989	1989	1989	1989
India	340	18.6	226	51.7	43	26.4	59	4.1	95
China	350	47.2	59.1	236.1	69	9.8	70	2.5	30
Pakistan	370	42.2	213	82.9	30	23.2	55	6.6	160
Sri Lanka	430	.91.4	173	109.4	87	17.8	71	2.5	20
Indonesia	500	122.3	263	106.8	74	35.2	61	3.3	64
Thailand	1220	1473	920	159.6	73	14.6	70	3.7	22
S. Korea	4400	1482	1832	392.0	N.A.	11.4	70	1.8	23
Average of poorest 41 countries (low income countries) of the world	330	40.7	33.0	80.2	56	20.2	62	3.9	70

Source: World Development Report 1991 Published by World Bank.

Table 2 brings out a more serious aspect of the failure of development process in India. It reveals that the annual rate of growth of GNP in India has been lower than in all other countries we have chosen for comparision since 1965. This implies that our country was not always the straggler among the Asian nations, but has gradually lagged behind others in the race of economic development over the last 30 years. Indeed, in 1965. India had ranked higher in per capita income than China, Pakistan, Sri Lanka and Indonesia but we have lost that position during the next 25 years.

Table 2 : Selected Growth rates (Country-wise)

Countries	Average Annual Growth-rates of per Capital GNP (%)	Agricultural Production %	Manufacturing (%)	Exports (%)
	1965-89	**1980-89**	**1980-89**	**1980-89**
India	1.8	2.9	7.3	5.8
China	5.7	6.3	14.5	11.5
Pakistan	2.5	4.4	7.9	8.5
Sri Lanka	3.0	2.2	6.2	6.7
Indonesia	4.4	3.2	12.7	2.4
Thailand	4.2	4.1	8.1	12.8
Malaysia	4.0	3.9	8.0	9.8
South Korea	7.0	3.3	13.1	13.8
Average of Poorest 41 Countries (low income countries) of the world	2.9	4.0	11.5	5.2

Source: World Development Report 1991 published by the World Bank.

During the 80s India was able to achieve a growth rate in agriculture and manufacturing which was lower than every other country except Sri Lanka, whereas the growth rate of her exports was lowest except in the case of Indonesia. The bottom line of table 2 reveals that except for exports in 1980s, India's GNP agriculture and industries have in fact been growing slower than even the average of the 41 low-income countries of the world. This means that India is not only near the tail end of the field already, but is falling even further behind.

We may look at any other points by which one gauges the ability of a country to manage its affairs e.g., the rate of rail, road and air accidents per thousand vehicle-kms, industrial accidents in relation to mandays of work, state of management of educational and other social institutions, average delay in disposal of cases in courts banks and the like, efficiency of functioning of public offices, maintenance of public facilities, sanitation and conservancy, ability to attract tourists, environmental management and creation of a sense of the social responsibility and civil sense in the average citizen. Each of these will confirm a dismal state of affairs in India.

India, Eastern Region and Bihar

Things however would start looking different if we lower our sights and confine our vision within INDIA. A regional comparision within this country would indicate that the North, South and West have been performing quite well in relation to the Eastern region of the country.[3] Within the Eastern region again, Bihar's performance has been poor in relation to major neighboring states. This comes out clearly if we place some indicators of Bihar against those of other larger Indian States, relatively smaller states from other regions and finally the major neighbouring states of the Eastern region. These indicators are given in three parts in Table 3.[4]

Table

It is clear from part 1 of table 3 that in comparision to the five other larger (in terms of population) states of India. Bihar ranks the lowest in almost every criterion. She is at the bottom in terms of per capita income, literacy rate, per capita power consumption, per capita production of foodgrains, milk and factory products and per capita bank credit. She has the highest percentage of rural population below poverty line, least number of hospital beds for every unit of population and largest deficit in electricity supply, Proportion of her population engaged daily in factory employment is lowest expect for U.P. while the percentage of her villages connected with all weather road and the rate of her fertilizer consumption per hectare is less than every other large-state except Madhya Pradesh.

Part II of the Table shows that in relation to the selected (somewhat) smaller states of southern, northern and western region. Bihar not only trails others in terms of almost every indicator, but that the gap between her and others is generally wider in this case. Except the fact that Rajasthan

3. An alternative perception would be that the Hindi speaking region (consisting of Bihar, Uttar Pradesh, Madhya Pradesh & Rajasthan) has been the laggard in relation to other regions and Bihar rnakes lowest within that region. The possible validity of this perception cannot be ruled out.

4. It would have made our comparision more accurates if the data of U.P. could be bifurcated between Eastern U.P. and WESTERN U.P. The former would be regarded as part of the Eastern region while the latter would have been considered, to be a part of northern Region along with Delhi, Punjab & Haryana. This would have also allowed us to evaluatee the alternative perception (see footnote 3) with greater veracity. In absence of such bifurcation, I have treated the whole of U.P. to be a part of Eastern region, though that is somewhat less accurate.

Table-3 Basic Development Indications (State-wise)

	Per Capita income (Rs.) 89-90	Per Capita-else con sumption (kwh)	Per hect Fert. con-sumption (kg.)	Liter-acy rate (%)	Popu-below poverty line (%)	Per Capita Gross Factory Output (Rs.)	Per Capita foods Gains Produc-tion	Per Capita milk availa-bility (kg./yr)	Daily factory employ % popu-lation	Per Capita Bank credit (Rs.)	Vill-ages conne-cted with all whether roads (%)	Popu per hospi-tal bed	Deficit in power supply (%)
	89-90	90-91	90-91	1991	87-88	82-83	82-83	90-91	1988	3/1991	87-88	1991	90-91
	1	2	3	4	5	6	7	8	9	10	11	12	13
All India	42.91	253	72.4	52.1	29.9	1971	186	64.3	19	1570	40.7	1316	7.9
Bihar	2122	109	56.8	38.5	40.9	1013	117	35.8	6.0	429	1315	2557	28.7
Part-I													
Maharashtra	6134	425	66.4	63.1	29.2	46.6	153	43.5	16.9	3801	52.9	667	3.9
U.P	3072	168	90.1	41.7	35.1	1080	217	72.3	4.5	673	42.8	2083	10.6
A.P	3211	261	133.2	45.1	31.7	1516	196	46.5	9.9	13.73	43.0	1613	7.9
M.P.	2778	254	35.4	43.5	36.7	1333	234	72.7	7.3	786	23.4	2778	2.5
W.B.	3963	144	90.3	57.7	27.6	1795	124	44.3	14.5	1514	41.4	1250	9.2
Part-II													
Punjab	7081	617	171.2	57.1	7.2	4071	763	254.7	17.5	2201	98.8	1299	1.1
Rajasthan*	2923	200	23.9	38.8	24.4	1073	207	100.4	5.9	713	21.2	2000	2.1
Gujarat	5404	463	64.9	60.9	18.4	4245	133	84.4	16.7	1699	73.6	758	4.1
T.N.	3894	319	115.1	63.7	32.8	3047	119	60.9	14.7	2438	63.2	1136	6.4
Karnataka	4075	291	66.3	56.0	32.1	1547	171	53.7	12.8	1844	32.9	1299	22.9
Kerala	3389	183	84.4	90.6	17.0	14.66	51	56.6	9.2	1570	100.0	413	0.5

Part-III													
U.P.	3072	168	90.1	41.7	35.1	1081	217	72.3	4.5	673	82.8	2083	10.6
W.B.	3963	144	90.3	57.7	27.6	1795	124	44.3	14.5	1514	41.4	1250	9.2
Orissa	3066	254	20.9	48.6	44.7	990	197	14.8	4.3	664	15.1	2273	22.0
Assam	3179	85	10.5	53.4	22.8	838	128	24.6	4.0	501	64.6	1754	N.A.

*Related to the year 1988-89

Source: Statistical outline of Indian 1992-93, Pub. Tata Services Ltd., Bombay.

has even less fertilizer consumption rate (quite understandably so), great proportion of villages not connected by all weather roads and marginally lower factory employment ratio than Bihar, while Kerala has lower foodgrain production per head and Karnataka marginally less villages connected by all weather roads, every state is far ahead of Bihar in every sphere of activity.

From **Part III** of the Table, we find that within the Eastern region, Bihar is still below all other states in per capita income, literacy rate, shortage of electricity and hospital beds as well as per capita availability of foodgrains and bank credit. But her performance in other areas does not compare unfavorably with others. In per capita power consumption, Bihar ranks higher than Assam. In fertilizer consumption rate, she is better off than Orissa and Assam. Same is the position with regard to per capita factory production and milk consumption. In daily factory employment rate, Bihar was better placed than U.P. Assam and Orissa. Orissa also had a lower percentage of village accessible by road throughout the year and in 1987-88, she also had a higher percentage of rural population below poverty line.

Table 3 also reveals that the gap between Bihar and the Part III states (i.e., Eastern Indian States) is generally narrower than that between her and the Part II or Part I States. (i. e. some what smaller states is Northern Eastern and Southern States, as well as the other largest states in the country).

In **Table 4** where Bihar's growth rate of foodgrains production and of agricultural production as a whole are compared with those of other regions and states on the same basis as in Table 3, same relative trends emerge as before viz., Bihar's the worst performer but her picture is less cheerless when compared with other states of Eastern region than when it is held against states from other regions of India. Relative yields of rice and foodgrains further confirm the trends, barring inevitably minor variations here and there.

Failure is wider than in rural development

It is important to appreciate that the trends we have noted are applicable not only to rural development indicators, but also to the indicators of industrial development (e.g. volume and growth rate of industrial production, generation of industrial employment, productivity of factory labour, generation of electricity, quality control and cost of production availability of institutional credit, incidence of industrial sickness etc.) social development (e.g. literacy, fertility rates, age of marriage, health care indexes, infant mortality rates, incidence of castisem, dowry and other social evils, sanitation and cleanliness etc.). Urban development (availability and growth rate of housing availability of other civil amenities and services, index of unlawful constructions index of planned as low growth and land utilization norms etc. educational development (i.e.) standards of higher education, academic attainments, games and sports, literacy and journalistic publication etc.), moral development (e.g. incidence of corruption, black money, tax evasion, administrative and political responsiveness, crime-rate, crimenalisation of political operatives etc.) and infrastructure management (maintenance of roads, transport system etc.); some of these yardsticks we have already included in Tables above while the rest may be easily studied. They would all point to a situation of India floundering at the near the bottom of the world and Bihar struggling at the bottom of India.

The True Nature of the Failure

The graduation of sluggishness that occurs through India, her eastern states and Bihar, along with its all pervasive character, suggests two things. First, Development is a Ladder-Phenomenon. Bihar undoubtedly stands on its lowest rung, but other Indian states are gradually dispersed only a little higher. They too are struggling way down the ladder while contestants in the form of other countries have generally climbed higher and are doing so faster. Second, to understand the phenomenon, looking merely at rural development or any other aspect in isolation could be grievously misleading. We have to look at the overall picture and search for that source of loss of society's vitality which may explain the total phenomenon of social inertia.

Failure of Motivation, Nation-building and Human Progress

Judging from all embracing character, it is clear what we are witnessing in India in general and Bihar in particular is thus essentially a Failure of Human Progress, a debility of human spirit. Extent of this failure may be more in some segments of society and so are its corresponding manifestations in the shape of development indicators. But it is certainly the retardation of human progress, the lack of progress in man's character and spirit, vitality and zeal, awareness, boldness self-confidence and national pride that is expressed through his myriad failures. Experience of different societies

Table 4 : -Foodgrains and Agricultural and Growth Rates (Inter state)

	Annual growth rate of foodgrain production (1961-62 to 82-83%)	Annual growth rate of agriculture production (1969-70 to 83-84%)	Foodgrain yield per hectare (kg.) (1982-82)	Yield of per hectare (kg) (1982-83)
	1	2	3	4
All India	2.4	2.20	1041	1230
Bihar	0.8	0.49	816	681
Part-I				
Maharashtra	1.9	5.59	677	1311
U.P.	2.8	3.19	1322	1115
A.P.	2.3	3.31	1274	2110
M.P.	1.0	1.65	696	711
W.B.	1.3	0.91	1043	1018
Part-II				
Punjab	6.3	3.92	2829	314
Rajasthan	1.9	2.47	651	750
Gujarat	3.9	3.92	923	1027
Tamilnadu	0.4	1.12	1245	1859
Karnataka	2.4	2.44	936	1916
Kerala	1.0	0.23	1593	1640
Part-III				
U.P.	2.8	3.19	1322	1115
W.P.	1.3	0.91	1043	1018
Orissa	1.3	2.28	730	1121
Assam	2.3	N.A.	1080	1121

Source: 1. Compiled from Basic Statistics relating to Indian Economy, EMIE Bombay, September, 1982

2. Selected Plan Statistics of Bihar 1986, Bihar State Planning Board, Patna.

at different periods of history tell us that save in exceptional instances, when a society starts PRODUCING WORTHY MEN that man's progress gets reflected in many faces of the social mirror. Economic development is but one face of it.

Inadequate appreciation of this basic truth leads us to mistake the image in one mirror to be the cause of that is another. Every event in the universe has a proximate cause, but the latter has its own proximate cause elsewhere. A logical chain of questions and answers would probably be like the following:

- Why don't industries run successfully in Bihar?
- Because of chronic shortage of power
- Why is there chronic shortage of power here?
- Because the Bihar State Electricity Board (BSEB) is reeking in inefficiency and corruption.
- Why is BSEB so corrupt and inefficient?
- It is because of the protection of corrupt politicians and the lack of political will.
- Why do you allow such policies to rule?
- Because voters are not conscious enough and elections bring forth only such men.

The chain of such causal queries (which no doubt could be prolonged indefinitely without any agreement) would invariably end up pointing towards failure of consciousness and man's spirit for betterment. Admittedly life of society is so complex that almost everything depends on everything else in its matrix, and a simple uniliner cause and effect chain would be too simplistic. Nevertheless, all reasonable queries generally converge on the same prime factor. If that prime factor is not influenced, attempts to steer the process by intervening at subsequent stages can have only limited or temporary effect.

Lack of human progress in a society implies the RETARDATION OF ITS AVERAGE MAN. If the average man of a society is awakened, if he acquires awareness, self-confidence, integrity and desire for progress, that society moves ahead. History is replete with evidence that the basic clues to a society's progress are the MOTIVATION, INSPIRATION AND SPIRIT of its average man.

A motivated man alone would show diligence, perseverance, courage, confidence, initiative and commitment. Only an inspired man would be ready to take risks, face challenges and make sacrifices. Only such a man would be, so to say, fired with a zeal to see things, improve for himself and for others around him. Contrarily, a man who has nothing to motivate or inspire him would in all likelihood suffer from timidity, lethargy, purposelessness, diffidence and subservience. Influenced by degrading 'tamaas' such a person would manipulate rather than work hard and would look for short-cuts which do not exist. The key to a society's progress lies therefore in the degree of motivation and inspiration of its average man. The rate of social transformation varies directly in proportion it.

To identify the causes of retardation of rural development in Bihar therefore, one must locate THE FACTORS THAT HAVE ADVERSELY AFFECTED THE MOTIVATION/INSPIRATION OF THE AVERAGE INDIAN IN RELATION TO OTHER COMPARABLE COUNTRIES, WHY THESE FACTORS ACQUIRED GREATER FORCE IN EASTERN INDIA IN GENERAL AND BIHAR IN PARTICULAR, AND WHAT MITIGATED THEIR IMPACT IN CASE OF SOME OTHER STATES.

Our scholars and researchers should address themselves to these questions rather than blaming one symptom of a desease for another.

The role of inspiring and motivating the average man does not rest on the rural masses, or the urban masses for that matter. This is the role of the elite, the leaders, rulers, law givers and policy-makers of the society. Conduct and actions of these elements of society combined with the long term effects of history are the determining factors of the motivation and spirit of the average man.

It is not fashionable to quote Swami Vivekananda on an economic topic, but the Swami had apparently perceived the process of social transformation clearly. Therefore, in his--'My Plan of Campaign' speech at Madras, wherein he explained how he proposed to build a new India, he said "Men, men, these are wanted; everything else will be ready, but strong vigorous believing young men sincere to the backbond are wanted". Indeed, economic development is but a natural outcome of the process of nation building and essence of nation-building is man-making. Unfortunately, Marxist and Nehruist writers lose sight of this basic perspective. As a result, they get lost in search of illusory economic causes, for failure of 'rural development'.

Suggested Approach for Further Enquiry

To understand the factors that have adversely affected the motivation, inspiration and spirit of Indian as a whole, and of some states more than others require considerable indepth research. We have to study our history not only of the British period, but of the 700 years that preceded and 47 years that followed it. We have to scan the pages of our history of the post-Somenath and post-Tryst with Destiny periods just as carefully at the post-Plassey period, if we want to locate the sources of damage to the average Indian's motivation, his loss of inspiration his sense of rootlessness and drift, his self-alienation and his fatalism. We have to objectively consider WHAT KIND OF STATE THAT HAS RULED OVER US during these periods, the IDEOLOGICAL FRAMEWORK within which they worked, the BASIC NATIONAL POLICIES they adopted, the NATIONAL ETHOS they tried to cultivate, the attitude they adopted towards their subject, and the long-term effect these had in the psyche of the people of this country and in different parts.

Instead of contenting ourselves with a critique of the British permanent settlement, we would need to study the agrarian and fiscal politicies of rulers like Alauddin Khilji and Firoz Tughlaq and their impact on Gangetic plains, Rajasthan and the rest of the country. We have to refer to the well recorded accounts of economic and agricultural impoverishment of this country in the medieval period, the cathartic damage suffered by human spirit in India during that time, and their lingering effects if any. We have to analyse the impact on Indian National mind of the regime of falsehood, unreality and hyped up ideas that was inaugurated with our 'Tryst-with-Destiny'. We have to delve deeper to understand why the de-motivating forces could not work as rigorously on some other states (like Punjab, Gujarat, Maharashtra or deep-South States) as they did in Bihar or Eastern U.P. or what counteracted these factors at some stage or other.

It would be logical to analyse all this in this article. Then only the article could be considered complete but that would take us much more than another full article in itself. I would therefore rest content just to place my hypothesis, and leave it to the readers to ponder, debate and form their own opinion for further study on these lines.

5. It would be quite possible for one to substitute 'Hindi Speaking region' for the 'Eastern region' and pursue the enquiry on that basis (see footnote 3). Indeed it is possible that there have been separate debilitating factors that accentuated the de-motivational causes in case of the Hindi speaking region and the Eastern regions. It is interesting to note that Eastern U.P. and Bihar are the only areas which are both part of the Hindi-belt and the Eastern region. Once the accentuating factors are indentified for both, one may find that Bihar and Eastern U.P. have suffered from the greatest degree of torpor simply because both sets of accentuating factors have operated in their case.

The Constraints to Evolution A Proper and Effective Health Service: An Appraisal

B.D. Prasad and
Narendra Prasad

The pre-requisite for this discussion on the above subject is the acceptance that the existing Health service is improper and ineffective.

The present scenario is that million become blind because of nutritional avitaminosis, and other million suffer and die unnecessarily, because of totally preventable Gastro-intestinal maladies. Infections, like tuberculosis, tetanus, diptheria, whooping cough etc., abound due to prolonged ill health because of malnutrition and anemias. All these continue to be potent threat to life and living.

Why has this happened? The answer obviously is not simple.

The main emphasis of our approach will be a plea for reappraisal of the expressed objectives of Health Care, its planning and execution.

The main reason for inadequacy and failure to healthy growth of any social delivery system is not mainly lack of organisation and proper Infrastructure.

Man is at the centre of creation of both wealth and health. Our failure on both the counts has been primarily due to socio-political thinking that India could be transformed through executive power into a great and strong Nation.

A brief analysis of vision and strategy pursued since the initiation of rural Health Programmes in mid fifties illustrates not much fault in the vision because how else could modern health technology be expanded in Rural India except through introduction of people and personnel equipped in this technology. But studies and assessment of temper and talent of the people who were introduced in this environment reveals that the doctors and others were alien to the environment to which they were introduced.

Let us do a research through a questionnaire of the experiences of doctors and health workers of the time and benefit from their experiences.

We happened to be among the early entrants into this system. Our experiences may be subjective. They need to be verified objectively.

Through illustrations, we shall try to establish, the followings:-

1. Vision of the health and the role of Doctors in rural health were usually absent. Medical curriculum did not prepare us for these.
2. Rural society was neither prepared nor was taken into confidence in planning and execution of the programmes.
3. The bureaucrats and mechanical objectives set for evaluation bore no relationship to the vision. Illiteracy, superstition and vested interest provided stumbling blocks to change.
4. Community health and social hygiene were ignored.
5. Delivery of PREVENTIVE and positive health-needed a technological understanding by the deliverer and the recipient neither were ready nor equipped.

Family Planning, Tuberculosis/Leprosy Control and etc.

Food, Nutrition, and other health care programmes.

The vision of a reconstructed health system was part of extension philosophy conceived by Sri S.K. Dey in early fifties. This vision relied heavily on an American experience which brought about significant rural development, when dedicated young educated individuals were involved in backward situations.

He himself is reported to have achieved phenomenal results in certain areas where he collected enthusiasts to bring about transformation of village communities.

This impressed the powers that be-and it became the driving force and norm for health planning.

Looking at this forty years later the present position regarding rural Health could be analysed as follows:

On the Positive Side:

1. There are six to ten qualified medical practitioners posted in development blocks covering a population of two to three lakhs.
2. Population within these areas has increased three fold--Increase in population (+) ve or (-) ve.
3. Small Pox has been eradicated.
4. Major epidemics are contained.
5. There is an infra-structure, which is in place at rural level.

On the Negative Side

1. The medical personnel are usually a dissatisfied lot--thus their efficiency in delivering services suffers.
2. The population is increasing in an uncontrolled fashion. The extension programmes did not succeed in convincing people for a planned family.
3. There is emerging trend for re-appearance of killer diseases caused by persistence and neglect of ordinary laws of sanitation.
4. The infrastructure although well expanded, creating under all pervasive inefficiency and corruption.

Under aegis of our institute the following need special attention that (1) whether the introduction of extension vision was without adequate understanding of Indian realities?

(2) In depth study of the real objectives and aspirations of the Men on ground is a must. Since, this in our view is the key to development and (3) to suggest, correctives where necessary or to suggest a complete rethinking.

Please permit us to be a little subjective. As we have already, said, we were among the early entrants into village environments.

In 1957, over 200 hundred doctors were posted in C.D. Blocks. Most of us did report to our bases and stayed there for upto three to eight years.

We have carried out a brief survey amongst the graduates of Patna Medical College, who graduated between 1954, 1955 and 1956.

Approximately two hundred and fifty doctors from this period entered the service. Today over thirty of them are eminent surgeons and physicians in Bihar. At least 30% of them hold high professional degrees and diplomas and are very successful by any standard.

The general impression about their experiences is not unpleasant, but certainly of unnecessarily wasted years which neither contributed to their own careers nor to the community health.

As to changing the environment and bringing medical science to people, they frankly admit failure for various reasons.

These include bureaucratic interference, people's ignorance and meagre resources-men and material others in a large measure. We tend to agree with them, but we must confess, this subject needs greater in depth study.

It is important to do this, because work at faulted approach will not be possible to achieve the goals and vision that we aspire.

* Served in C.D. Blocks from 1958 to 1965 and thereafter worked and practised in U.K. as consultant. I Orthopadic Surgeon, is now based at Patna.

** Served in C.D. Blocks from 1958 to 1961. After his return from U.K. was associated with medical teaching and surgical practice. Retired as Professor and Head of Department PMCH and is now based at Patna.

Let us look at rural India that we woke upto in 1947.

With all the hope about our glorious cultural past, the reality in 1947 was as Sumitranandan Pant has vividly expressed in "**Gramya**":

''कोटि- कोटि संतप्त नग्न तन,
अशिक्षित, निर्बल, निरस्त्र जन''

This cruel destiny was not accidental, nor evolutionary, but was the result of a planned and systematic plunder and exploitation of the resources and planned effort to destroy the cultural heritage and indeginus assets.

Discussion on this would be a different subject, but the view that we take, is that the prolonged presence of a foreign irritant had manifold effects. One of them was the creation of a compradol class, who were anglophils. In their vision of India of future, they saw Indian: as Black Europeans. This was their view of modernity whatever be the rights or wrongs of this vision, they neither cared nor carried conviction with the Indian masses.

Our bureaucracy largely constituted of this class though anatomically Indian, they never had any respect for the masses.

The practitioners of modern medicine were no different. By the time a medical man became professionally efficient, he had nothing but disrespect for the Indian systems of medicare and practice.

Here lay the crux. The Doctor was not one of the community as was the Hakim or Vaidya or even a quack in the village.

Thus, though we were effective in a crisis, epedimics or serious illnesses but not in teaching them the laws of community care or sexual matters. We had neither an understanding of the problem nor much conviction.

Should not we find out what people expect from medical men. Miracles or scientific health care?

Also from doctors, do they want only to achieve technical excellence, to do the impossible or relieve the day to day problems by becoming, friend, philosopher and guide of the society?

Is it possible to carry out this exercise?

Friends, it is only possible after we admit that the greatest failure in perception of constraint, is the "human factors".

The inhumaneness of the medicare springs from unbelonging and disinheritance from the community.

I- Decentralisation--Vs. Centralisation

A- Every Block should appoint its own medical team.

Note: Transfer and Posting by a central authority is a bureaucratic practice to keep a control by a superior authority. We must recognise that community medicine is different and requires talent of a different type.

Here we suggest a complete overhaul and initial a change of philosophy from the recruitment of medical personnel onwards.

(1) The entrant is made to commit himself to community medicine. And as in the case of Armed Forces his training is tailored to the needs of rural community, COMPULSION--but choice is made in advance.

(2) Community sponsored candidates, different communities should have programme of their own and those candidates with local commitments and responsibility. They should have their own method of exercising control.

There should be a fair degree of interchangeability commensurate with individual and social ambitions and needs respectively.

These should be initiated without prejudice to the existing pattern, so that unnecessary conflict of vested interests with newer patterns are muted.

Besides, we are tempted to compare medicare's science and practice as an example to compare the role of centralisation and decentralisation.

As a science, understanding of ill health is central to all training. One understands a disease as system based/caused to an organ or an infection and the likes and treatment is devised accordingly.

But when treating a patient, if one were to convert a human being to typhoid of fracture--disaster sets in. One does not treat a disease who happens to be a human being, a human individual, who is ill.

Taking this analogy further, our premises would be that vision of universal health (the science and technology of medicare) should be centralised but execution (practice of medicare) should be decentralised as we do in any understanding related to scientific discipline.

Commitment to community is a must and it takes a lifetime. That is why a G.P. in village is more effective socially than others.

The argument against this is the lure of glory by some who seek technical excellence. This can be done by providing channels for them separately. But they must offer their choices and compete for them. The existing option of advanced medical institutes gives them this option.

Spread of talent on all fronts is essential and the hallmark of choice must be the individual's competence and communities trust in him.

B. Central Authority's power should be limited to quality control, guidance, conduct and ethics and other related.

C. A strong overseeing inter-action machinery should be set up, for imparting information mutually beneficial to corresponding communities and specialised knowledge.

D. Frequent work-shops should be made essential and profitable parts of continuing medical education.

E. People should be asked to question and an informed discussion with the patient must be a part of consultation. In other words both the people and doctors bring the medicare to earth from the mystic miracle making art to the level of knowledge and science.

II. Redefinition of objectives and targets. At present from the moment a prospective doctor enters the medical schools, his objective is to achieve mastery in the art of healing by targeting the ill. His courses of study proceed from a normal and healthy individual to the diseased and then to restoration of health.

In societies, where pre-existing organisation has imparted an ethical norm, it does not matter because there exists a practice which can be enforced by Medical councils or the likes.

In India, where professional bodies have involved differently and the bureaucratic set up has precluded direct service practices vis-a-vis mass--it is imperative that professional bodies and representative bodies of masses should come together and build a curriculum of medical education, where the objective is not simply the ill patient, but illness itself.

III. While respecting the sentiments expressed in Health for all by 2000 A.D., one has not to be a cynic to say that this is a heap of rubbish indulged by populist politicians.

Conditions of health and illness are in perpetual motion. As societies evolve newer and more exacting demands are made from its scientists and medical men.

There are limitless mileage to be covered beyond the horizon, but that does not either mean that we sit back and let things pass by nor to accept an absurd demand and work for it.

Our immediate objective in India should be limited to an obtainable proportion. If we achieve clean drinking water and prevent deaths by communicable diseases by the year 2000, along with a reasonable population growth rate, it will be a remarkable achievement.

•

Factors Retarding Rural Development

Shree Shankar Sharan.

What Holds up Rural Development is Lack of Adequate will and Organisation in the Rural Sector.

There are many areas in the country where the farmer have got organised and by their collective strength can dictate terms to the Government. In U.P. we have a powerfully organised farmers movement under Tikait, who is a grass root leader. In Maharashtra there is a powerful farmer's lobby under Sharad Joshi. In Bihar too there was a strong Kisan Andolan under Sahajanand Saraswati. Somehow after the abolition of Zaminadari and the Land Ceiling Act, the elite has turned its attention away from the problems of farmers except of course the Naxalites who by violent methods have continued to wage a struggle for the emancipation of small farmers and landless labourers. Some good work has been done by individuals including a foreigner to highlight the man made problems of unupdated land records, nonentry in the records of under-tenants and problems of insecurity of tenure.

The co-operative movement which could do a great deal to deal with problems of fragmentation and agricultural credit at affordable interest rates has been captured and corrupted by a Mafia which is an urban rural combine. The problems of agricultural credit, for long captive to usurious money lenders has merely changed hands to equally unscruplous, exploitative and corrupt men of the cooperative movement. Violence directed at big farmers and counter violence has tended to divide the rural community and disrupt rural peace and rural development, though they have made some long term gains i.e. higher rural wages. The burden on the farmer continues to be heavy. He is no longer enthused by the Naxalite movement.

Bank finance in the priority sectors is also picking up corruption apart from being selective, harassing and boorishly impersonal and a replica of colonial attitudes.

The development administration does not directly dispense finance except during natural calamities. Even if it did, its image of corruption is no less, murky.

The rural infrastructure has both expanded and dwindled. There are more roads now than before independence and better, though still overcrowded transport facilities. The links between the producer and the market have improved. So has the flow of information.

Power, however, whose only provider is the state has all but vanished. This has harmed both agriculture and the farmers will to improve. Power run pumps do not run, most of the time. Farmers cannot enjoy many of the perks of modern living after improving their economic status, without power. Lack of power is turning farmers to the more expensive diesel. Many have changed from electric to diesel pumps. There has been an all round growth in food production inspite of an inefficient Government which does not match to govern.

The rural rich apart from buying tractors, sinking tubewells and using fertilizers and improved seeds do not invest enough in agriculture. They have not diversified either in the pattern of cropping, growing cash crops or in the agro-industries sector. The last is the big virgin field open for the enterprising farmer. He needs support in terms of information, willing and ready finance, helpful and unexploitative cooperative or banking structure and marketing facilities.

It is in these matters that the Government was expected to have a role which it continues to fail. The N.G. Os have also tried to fill the gap and should continue to do so but their numbers and spread is small and corruption is also seeping into them.

The multinational companies, if they can still come despite the political campaign against them derived from the memories of the East India Company though the days of imperialism are clearly over and big power intervention is no respecter of economic ties (as in Iraq) could provide or arrange finance. People who oppose MNCs should take into account the poor and unethical record of indegenous sugar mills. The MNCs, will need to earn people's credibility. Their terms for supplying seeds will need to go beyond Dunkel, not be conceived in arrogant and imperialist terms and be easy pragmatics and popular.

There is still chance for the co-operative movement. They have put the milk supply scheme on a sound footing in the very same North Bihar in which the other co-operatives have cheated and failed. The educated Youth have a chance to bring cooperative movement in a better shape.

Non-conventional energy, specially solar energy and renewable (e.g.

Gobar Gas) energy should be tried out for Cottage Industry. We should learn to be self-dependent in power.

The age old Textile industry should go back to villagers in the shape of Ambar Charkah and handloom.

Let the villages learn to live without the state in more and more areas.

That brings us to Panchayati Raj, yet to start in Bihar. The Panchayat should learn to use the power they have got and not lose them by disuse. There are many things they have not got like control over the police, as the countries do in England for which they should legitimately struggle in future. At the moment they should merely learn to use the power they have got.

Panchayati Raj is not a gift from the state to the people. It is returning to people what was theirs. Let us learn once again to be our Masters.

Lastly the ownership of land and security of tenure in a village is a vexed question. In the interest of higher production and larger investment there are those who want the Ceiling Act scrapped. Production as a result will undoubtedly increase but the small farmer will be bought out to become agricultural labourer.

There are others who would like a lower ceiling, I being one of them, so that land can be redistributed and each family own as near an acre of land as possible.

The third option is of Vinob's Gramdan in which all ownership vests in the village, though farming is done individually. Of the three the third is the most revolutionary and keeps the village land intact and safe for the villagers by prohibiting sale outside the village. But it does not change the disparity in nature of land use.

It is the duty of the political parties to press for one of these three models as part of their campaign. Let the rural people decide which model they prefer. Let each state also decide which model suits them and let states be different from one another.

On one issue we must all agree. The subdivision and fragmentation of land under the succession laws must stop. The law should be amended to provide that land can not be subdivided below 10 or 5 acres and must be held and farmed jointly.

•

Retarders of Rural Development in Bihar

Hans Kumar Sahay

The present paper seeks to analyse the main factors which have retarded the pace of rural development in Bihar. In this context following point have been kept in view:

In the first place, the concept of rural sector is inclusive of, but is wider than, the agricultural sector; agricultural sector is unquestionably the dominant component of the rural sector but non-agricultural sector is also to be taken into account from the angle of the attainment of the desired rural development. Industrial, commercial and service sub-sectors exist within the non-agricultural sector of the rural economy. It is the development of the rural sector in its entirety that is called for.

Secondly, 'development', a very comprehensive concept, has not only economic but not-economic dimensions too and between these dimensions, in reality, very complex relations exist. However, the analysis of development of the rural economy, in all its dimensions and complexity, though desirable for adequate comprehension of the issues involved and for formulation of more effective strategy for the realisation of the goal in view, is not feasible in this paper. Hence the scope of discussion in this paper is limited to only main factors which have slowed down the tempo of economic development of the rural segment of the economy of Bihar, a lagging state of India.

Economic development of the rural economy of Bihar, to be really effective, must be sustainable; it should be capable of maintaining its tempo endogenously so as to ensure on a continuous basis reasonably high rate of growth of output and employment in response to rising requirements of the whole economy, rural and urban, and further promote equitable distribution of the gains of development sectionally and spatially in particular, it should enable those who are below the poverty line to rise above it on a lasting basis. Such a sustainable development is attained where development promoting forces become stronger than development retarding forces durably; obviously, it takes time and involves sacrifice and hardwork and calls for in domitable will, political in particular and on the part of the people in general, to overcome the barriers in the path of development in this fashion.

Barriers are both subjective and objective in character. Subjective barriers are psychological variables, for example, the perceptions, the attitude, the will, the responses etc. of the individual taken alone or in group; all these variables are fundamental to development for, if favourably inclined, they accelerate development, if not, they do decelerate it. On the other hand, objective, barriers are related to availability of goods and services, for example, capital stock, road etc; their shortage retards, but their adequate availability, promotes development. Notably, the two, the subjective and the objective barriers are inter-related, they interact with each other. From the stand point of the choice of strategy of development, the important point to stress is that objective factors are more amenable to change in the shorter, span of time, whereas subjective conditions take longer period of time to undergo transformation. Hence in the formation of development strategy for immediate execution greater emphasis is laid on altering the former than the latter which is more time taking. In the discussion of the retarders that now follows, attempt is made to analyse those which are objective rather than subjective in character.

Underdevelopment Infrastructure in Rural Areas

It goes without saying that rural development at fast rate is impossible in the absence of adequate growth of infrastructural facilities in the areas; of these, irrigation, power and roads are looked upon as crucial to rural development.

Irrigation and Flood Control

That water is a critical input of agricultural production is indisputable. Provision of irrigation facilities so as to ensure assured supply of water to agricultural sector is highly significant for reduction of dependence of agricultural production on uncertain rainfall and for facilitating the modernisation of agriculture. In Bihar, despite planned efforts, according to the Draft Eighth Five Year Plan, assured irrigation covers only 46 per cent of the net cropped area. Cultivation, therefore, still remains dependent very largely on rainfall. The crop intensity has been more or less static at 1.35".[1] The scope for further expansion of irrigation facilities is wide in

Bihar. According to a Report, out of identified irrigation potential of 124 lakh hectares (65 lakh hectares under major and medium irrigation and 50 lakh hectares under minor irrigation projects) net irrigated areas by 1980-81 was only 29 lakh hectars.[2] Also, the Draft Eighth Five Year Plan of the State reveals the existence of wide scope of expansion in this regard in Bihar.

Major part of the North Bihar is badly affected by flood and of the South Bihar, not infrequently, by drought. In consequence the agricultural and rural development has been retarded in the State. Poor water management has been a key factor depressing the rural economy of Bihar.

Power

In rural areas, modenisation of agriculture, the much desired process designed to augment productivity, presupposes regular and adequate supply of commercial power at reasonable price. Further, rural industrialisation, an important ingredient of strategy of diversified rural development, also calls for such flow of power the rural segment. In fact, attempt to increase production and productivity significantly in both farm and non-farm sectors in the rural economy can not succeed without basic supportive façility in the form of power. Unfortunately, however, this infrastrure is highly under-developed, Power-poverty is indicated by a per capita installed capacity of 19.5 watts in the state against 65.2 watts for the country. Per capita consumption of power in Bihar in 1987-88 (99 KWH) was well below the national average (191KWH), power deficiency is an important factor slowing the pace of rural development in Bihar.

Inadequate investment in power sector, sluggish expansion of generating capacity, coupled with poor maintenance of the existing power plants, inadequate generation and inefficient distribution of power have contributed to the persistence of power poverty in Bihar, affecting adversely the pace of economic growth of Bihar as a whole and also its rural sector.

Roads

Both from angles of securing the supply inputs and disposal of the output which affect significantly the cost-benefit ratio of economic units and investment and production decision, adequate development of the transport, particularly of roads, is of paramount importance for rural development. The existing condition in Bihar, from this stand point, is quite unsatisfactory. The road length per lakh of population as on 31st March, 1990 was only 124 kms. in Bihar as against 211 kms. for All India and that of surfaced roads 49 and 101 kms. respectively. Further about 50 per cent of the roads actually constructed so far are kutcha. Such a state of roads has retarded rural development in Bihar.

Demographic Pressure and Inadequate Qualitative Improvement in Human Resources

The second most populous state in India Bihar has to support 10.2 percent of the population with merely 5.3 per cent of area of the country. The land-man ratio already averse is deteriorating further with increasing rate of growth of population. The decennial growth rate of population has been steadily rising over the last few decades, excepting the last one when it recorded a marginal fall, as will appear from the following Table.[3]

	1941-51	1951-61	1961-71	1971-1981	1981-91
Bihar	10.27	19.76	21.33	24.06	23.49

Increasing pressure of population has retarded rural development. Rapid population growth, combined with the operation of inheritance laws, is leading to a decline in average size of holding, as well as to an increase in fragmentation of holdings and is thereby accentuating rural poverty.[4]

This is the finding of a study with reference to poverty and income distribution in "Bangladesh" by Alamgir and Ahmed; it is pertinent to Bihar. Rapid growth of rural population retards rural development for it slows down the rate of growth in per capita income, an important determinant of rural household savings and investment and further increases the supply of rural labour force which for want of matching increase in opportunities for gainful employment, aggravates the problem of under-employment and unemployment in rural areas and contributes to agrarian unrest.

There is a qualitative dimension of rural population. Bihar has been lagging behind in general literacy and education and provision of health services. In 1991, only 38.54 per cent of population in Bihar was literate as against the national average of 52.11 per cent. The literacy of females was depressingly low at 23.10 per cent. The number of hospital beds available in Bihar was only 39 per lakh of population in 1986. Under development of human resources has also stood in the way of fresh development in Bihar.

Technological Backwardness

Application of improved technology is necessary to increase productivity in case not only of agriculture but industry in the rural sector. However, on account of lack of vigorous research for development of appropriate technology for small units which predominate in rural sector in Bihar, traditional techniques are used by most of these units which hinder the process of acceleration of growth of their output. The small and marginal farmers have large number in Bihar and those engaged in village and cottage industries suffer from this angle and their economic condition does not show any sign of desired improvement. As productivity remains low large number of landless workers in the rural areas also find their incomes depressed. The persistence of technological backwardness thus is a formidable stumbling block in the path of speedy development of the rural economy of Bihar.

Ineffectiveness of Institutions in the Rural Area

Among the institutional factors retarding rural development in Bihar, tardy implementation of land reforms, ineffective operation of institutions providing finance to rural sector, particularly to small productive units and weaker sections of the rural population, slow growth of the marketing institutions and unsatisfactory working of Panchayats, to name the new important area, have combined to slow down the pace of rural development in Bihar.

Lack of Efficient Rural Development Plan Implementing Machinery and People's Participation

An important retarder of rural development in the State of Bihar has been the lack of emergence of a specialised machinery designed to translate the plan for rural development into reality effectively. Bureaucratic machinery has its own intrinsic limitations in this regard. In the ultimate analysis, the sustainable and speedy development of the rural segment is attainable only with voluntary active and honest participation of the rural people in the formulation and execution of the Plan.

The preceding discussion has highlighted in brief, mainly economic factors; non-economic factors, however, are also important; social and above all, political factors are highly significant since all economic policies are decided at the top of the political level. It follows, therefore that the pace of rural development is also a function of the behaviour of the non-economic factors.

That retarders of rural development and in fact development of Bihar as a whole have been operative is unmistakably clear from studies of inter regional disparities in India. Rothermund, for example, has analysed, economic and social indicators of regional disparities in India and listed Bihar as a state featured by unredeemed backwardness in every respect coupled with rural poverty.[5] Bhalla also, in his article "Agrarian change in India since independence" states that from the view point of agricultural output during 1969-70 to 1983-84, it is the most pupulus states of Bihar and West Bengal that have shown the worst performance. The growth rate of agriculture during this period in Bihar and West Bengal was 0.49 and 0.9 per cent respectively.[6]

The problem of rural development, complex as it is, however, must not be analysed in isolation from, but in conjuction with, the problems of urban development and of the Indian economy as a whole and the same is true of the study of the retarders of rural development in Bihar.

References

1. Planning Development, Government of Bihar, 1992-93 Vol. 1, Chapter 1, P. III
2. Agricultural Productivity in Eastern India, Vol II Report of the Committee on Agricultural Productivity in Eastern India, Reserve Bank of India, 1984, P. 238
3. Draft Eighth Five Year Plan, cip. Chapter 1 p.i
4. 'Rural Poverty in South Asia' etc. by Srinivasan, T.N. and Bardhan P., Oxford University Press, second impression 1990, p.2
5. 'Regional Disparities in India', Rural and Industrial dimensions, ed. by Rothermund D. and Saha, S.K. Manohar, 1991, pp. 3-4
6. Economic development of India and China: A comparative study. Indian Council of Social Science Research, Lander International in Association with ICSSR, 1988. p. 14.

•

Socio-Economic Causes of the Dynamics in Rural Bihar

Priyadarshi

Whereas Punjab with an area of 50000 square Kilometer and 2 crore population contributed 11% of national foodgrains production during 1987-90 period, Bihar with much larger area of 174000 square Kilometer and much higher population of 8.6 crore could contribute only 6.9 per cent. About 40.8 per cent of population of Bihar was living below poverty line in 1987-88 while persons living below poverty line in Punjab accounted for only 7.2 per cent of its population.

Every year people from Bihar migrate to Punjab and Haryana, though its population is more than 4 times to that of Punjab and its area is more than three times to that of Punjab. Production and employment in Bihar can grow provided the available water and human resources are integratedly developed properly and adequately. Both productivity and growth of employment have to be given importance. Though the eight South East Asian countries popularly known as tigers have succeeded in raising their rate of growth higher than of other countries, but they have also not neglected the principle of equity in their development.

In the district of Gaya the peaceful continuous struggle for ten years has yielded 10,000 acres surplus land which has benefited 10000 families. This has led to their economic emancipation through increase in productivity and avenues of employment on an average the agricultural production has become double and in certain pockets it has recorded growth by three times. The second change has occurred in administrative system of the area. Borachatti and Mohanpur circles are backward, still they are competing with developed circles. Besides, the presence of non-traditional people in Block offices demanding their share in welfare programmes has changed the character of these offices.

Arun Sinha in his research analysis has visualilsed five collective forces working in this process of revolution.

One is Sangharsh Vahini of Bodh Gaya revolution, the other is naxals, the third is communist parties, fourth is tribal revolution and the fifth is revolutionary element in Christian Missions who believe in revolution Sociology.

In the famous book *'Social Origin of Democracy and Dictatorship"* Barringtan R. Moore has written two important aspects about India, one that like China it did not record agricultural revolution and second that in India the modern democracy has become static. He holds that the Indian Society is not only traditional and old but non-dynamic. In view of these factors Moore has visualised that the inter conflict of the Indian society may lead to the decay of democracy as a result of which the danger of dictatorship may emerge. The analyses of Moore made in sixties appears to have been contradicted by the decade of nineties, though the anticipation of Moore had proved correct a decade immediately after his writings. In a general view the society in Bihar appears to be in accordance with the analysis of Moore. But analysis of events appears to lead to rise of social inter conflicts along with democracy. Still the goal for a developing and dynamic social order based on modern democratic infrastructure and democratic culture is desirable.

The revolution of castes shape the social order without being unnerved with political leadership which has taken over these revolutions, its impact has to be analyised. The speciality of caste system that the downtrodden should remain absorbed in psychological combination and do not destroy the atrocities resulting from caste system in view of fear-psychosis of rebirth has now lost its significance.

Arvind Narayan Das in 1991 in his book 'The Republic of Bihar' has correctly picturised the change in production brought about through revolution in Bihar specially in areas of Patna, Nalanda, Gaya, Rohtas, districts and in Central Bihar. I want to confirm it from the changes arrived at in Chapra, Siwan and Gopalganj, Punjab farmers analysis the changes of market forces while attempting growth of agricultural production. But farmers in Bihar have only one goal namely to increase agricultural production--Bihar farmer is feeding more than half of the unemployeds in Bihar.

The literacy drive can increase the new aspirations in Bihar.

I have to make four suggestions:

1. The resolution of land reforms should be restrengthened,
2. The new provisions of Punchayati Raj should be implemented,
3. The sale purchase system of foodgrains should be strengthened in a manner to facilitate farmers to get at least 15% profit on the sale of their foodgrains,
4. The indigenous resources should be exploited for lift irrigation, electricity, roads, health care and education.

The English version of the original script in Hindi has been translated by Dr. H.K. Sinha.

24

Development of Bihar: Infrastructural Support

Pradhan H. Prasad

Bihar is the second most populous State in India. Since India has a form of government which is highly centeralised, the central plan for development has been playing a domineering role in the process of progress in all parts of the country since August 15, 1947 when the Indian National Congress, under a compromise with the British imperialism, got the power the rule transferred to itself. More than four decades have elapsed since then. The outcome of this process has been succinctly brought out in the cover story caption of the Illustrated Weekly, August 29--September 4, 1992. It reads as follows:

"India, they say, is a great country. Rich in minerals, richer in natural resources, lot of sun, lots of water. Its technical know how is excellent. India's computer engineers design software for US firms. The fifth largest technical force is matched by its fifth largest army. For a poor country, it has blasted off a good number of missiles, and has successfully tested an atom bomb. It is good, they say, in other areas too. Democracy for one, population for another. Why then is India the grandest failure"?

If Bihar and areas similar to it which as a whole are less advantageously placed than India are a shade more non-developed than the country taken together, there is nothing strange or surprising about it. It is what is expected in such a situational dynamics. Moreover, Delhi is considered as most developed state as it has the highest per capita income among Indian States. But then its 53 per cent population (highest among the cities in India) live in slums. Now the question is which is more non developed Bihar or Delhi?

As against Marxian goal of stateless society, Gandhi's dream was of a fully decentralised and democratic society. Gandhi has said that "independence must begin at the bottom. Thus, every village will be a republic or panchayat having full power".[1] In tune with the Indian Psyche, revolutionary Ram Prasad Bismil wrote three days before his hanging, i.e. on 16th December 1927, "Hanging has been fixed at 6.30 in the morning of 19th. There is nothing to worry about it. By the grace of God I shall be re-born many times and my objective shall be to attain complete freedom in the world, everybody shall have equal right on the gift of nature so that no one rules over other. Governance by Panchayats shall be universal".[2] Ram Manohar Lohia had also advocated a Panchayat system of governance under a federal structure for the solution of the problems related to minorities.[3] In a letter to Stafford Crips on 27th January 1946, Jawaharlal Nehru had written, "I suppose you know what the Congress has proposed from time to time to solve the communal problem. It has stated that there should be a federation of autonomous units with certain minimum list of compulsory common subjects. These have not been enumerated but presumably they will be defence, foreign affairs, communication, currency etc."[4] In spite of these preceptions which were not based on bookish knowledge but on erudition obtained in the process of struggle for social justice and against British imperialism, when Congress got power transferred to itself from the British imperialism on 15th August 1947, it instead of adopting a federal structure, provided for a strong central rule for a big country of 36 crore people living amidst innumerable variations in terms of religion, caste, race, language, ritual, culture etc. Such was the decline in the standard of wisdom that the Indian Constitution emerged as an artificed but attractive version of the Government of India Act of 1935 which was enacted to provide Indians with limited self government. The compradore character of Indian ruling class surfaced clearly.

This is not all. In his speach in Motiganj on the 30th November 1939, Jawaharlal Nehru had said, " The experience of past twenty-eight months has proved that the cadre of Indian Civil Service as a whole is absolutely incompetent and inefficient. This does not mean that there is no competent and expert man in the service, but the general body has proved its incompetence and I think, it is the most inefficient body of service in the world".[5] Still in the framework of the pact related to transfer of power, Jawaharlal Nehru retained this incompetent service which was compradore in character, by simply making slight change in its name from ICS to IAS. The process of bureaucratisation was speeded up.

Gandhi was opposed to the capitalist industrialisation which has evolved amidst the expansion of Eureocentric culture. In this context Gandhi had said that "to make India like England and America is to find some races and places on the earth for exploitation".[6] Ram Manohar Lohia's historical analysis of 1943 has provided him the basis to maintain in a forthright manner that imperialism has been an abiding feature of capitalism. According to him,

"Imperialism not only appears at the first stage of capitalism but goes on developing with it. Capitalism seeks its external dynamics, one might say, even before it is born and, insatiable in this search, it gobbles up one country after another"[7]. He further added that "in history so far there has been no capitalism without imperialism".[8] In spite of these perceptions, the Indian ruling class, under the leadership of Jawaharlal Nehru, became active in dynamising capitalist industrialisation. But in order to dupe the exploited Indian people, the entire development process was taken under state patronage alongwith the expansion of public sector in an effort to ape the Russians. Even during the period of imperialist's rule railways, post and telegraph service etc had been kept under state's sector to serve the purpose of exploitation by imperialism. Jawaharlal Nehru has said as early as in April 1929, "If we are to eradicate poverty, we must first do away with this widespread unemployment"[9]. Gandhi had maintained that prevailing unemployment had also been responsible for communal riots. Even with these perceptions the development plans accorded priority to accumulation and production and not to employment generation. Since the country to speed up the process of capitalised industrialisation, the process of internal colonisation gathered additional momentum in India. It is the process of Internal colonisation which generates the dualism of less non-developed and more non-developed areas existing side by side in an overall phenomena of non-development.

Bihar belongs to that part of the country which has been the worst victim of this intercolonizations. The uneven regional growth which sufraced with colonisation of this country by Great Britain, a maritime power, found the landlocked areas like Bihar neglected and most exploited. The situation instead of improving worsened further after India acquired neo-colonial status on August 15, 1947. The increasing pace of bureaucratisation concomitant middle person culture and lack of autonomy in matters of political economy of development, both at local and State levels, killed the local initiative and dormant wisdom of people which being region specific was denied to the country. With India finding itself now tropped in worst quagmire of non-development, chances of Bihar's progress appeares even more difficult.

The present government at centre has not only completed its five years term but has gone ahead with its New economic policy 1991. This policy was initiated formally when this government presented its first budget of 1991-92 on July 24, 1991. This policy which is also known as a policy associated with 'libralisation' make a turning point in the economic history of India as it assigned a much greater role for the "market forces' in the context of economic dynamics of the country than hither to existed. The progressive removal of bureaucratic controls, it was argued, would release the market forces to promote competition and concomitant efficiency in the domestic production process. In this process, priority was accorded to considerably liberalisation of imports and relaxation in foreign exchange control. The propoganda base for this priority was that it would encourage inflow of foreign capital which is the need of the hour for development of a capital scare country such as India.

What was forgotten was that India has been technologically dependent for its capitalist development since long on imports at an increasing pace. Since 1948, this dependence manifested itself in foreign trade deficit, foreign indebtedness and foreign debt servicing at an over increasing rate. This began to exert downward pressures on value of rupee, both externally and internally, and domestic rates of profit. This in turn encouraged outflow of capital associated also with a wide verity of clandestine transfers rather than inflow of capital from abroad . It was to protect the Indian economy from these adverse impacts that import restrictions and foreign exchange control were initiated after the end of British colonial rule. But as soon as these restriction and control were relaxed, the forces retarding India's development came into full play.

There was a more sharp decline in the international value of rupee in the post New Economic Policy (Post NEP) era as compared to the pre-New Economic Policy (Pre NEP) period. The rate of average annual rupee value of US dollar has increased to 14 per cent during post NEP period of five years (i.e. 1991-92 to 1995-96) as compared to 8 per cent in the pre-NEP five years period (i.e. 1986-87 to 1990-91). The inflow of foreign capital which amounted to a total of Rs. 55951 crores during 1986-87 to 1990-91 has declined to a level of Rs. 35739 crores, a decline of about 36 per cent, during the same five years periods. This has happened in spite of the fact that with the initiation of 'liberalisation' policy, many allurements were offered to foreign investors and numerous memoranda of understanding (MOU) were signed in a coremonial manner with great fan-fare. The domestic capital formation as a percentage to Net National Product has declined from about 18.9 per cent in earlier five years period to about 17.3 per cent during the five years period after the initiation of the New Economic policy. That is why the latter five years period witnessed a lower annual average growth rate in manufacturing and Gross Domestic Product than the earlier five year period. The average annual growth rate declined from about 8 per cent during 1986-87 to 1990-91 to about 5 per cent during 1991-92 to 1995-96 in 'manufacturing, construction, electricity, gas and water supply' and about 6.1 per cent to 4.5 per cent in Gross Domestic Product. In spite of significant reduction in currency expansion and deficit budgetting by the centre, the wholesale prices have been rising at an annual average rate of about 10 per cent in latter period than about 8 per cent in earlier five years period.

However, it may be possible to pick some figures for some years to show positive gains arising on account of New Economic Policy 1991. For example, it can be suggested that since rise in wholesale price index has declined from about 10.85 per cent in 1994-95 to about 7.39 per cent in 1995-96 rise in prices would decline further in 1996-97 and thereafter. It can also be suggested that the impact of the New Economic Policy has taken some more than expected time to fructify but that the signs are hopeful. But then this type of myths get exploded when one examines the fact that rise in wholesale price index declined from 10.06 per cent in 1992-93 to about 8.35 per cent in 1993-94 and than it rose again. Similar is the situation regarding proportion of poor in the population when we resort to such half-truths.

It was the mounting pressure of our external debt, debt servicing and foreign deficit which brought us to accept the ***diktat*** of the world Bank and IMF which forms the core of the New Economic Policy 1991. These continue to increase unabated and the future continues to be depressing as is obvious from the following table:

Year	External debt March-End	Foreign debt service payments	Foreign Trade Deficit
1990-91	163001	16116	10645
1991-92	252910	20191	3810
1992-93	380746	25419	3810
1993-94	290418	25986	3350
1994-95	311792	34343	7297
1995-96	350000*		13379*

*Approximation

But then the nation still hopes for better days ahead. All parties including even the left accept the spirit of New Economic Policy if not explicitly at least implicitly. What a grand level of ignorance! Even the intellingentia who are supposed to know and analyse facts are as ignorent as the illiterate masses. Are we not supposed to look before we leap?

Imperialism, since its presence in the Indian sub-continent has always succeeded in its machination to keep India either a colonial or a neo-colonial region where non-development will be its abiding feature with some areas remaining less non-developed and other areas like Bihar remaining more non-developed. The mechanism of exploitation that gathered momentum after India acquired a neo-colonial status (i.e., after August 15, 1947) consisted mainly of growing adverse terms of foreign trade, ever increasing profits and interest earned by multinational companies and foreign creditors from the imperialist nations. These are well established facts which became unmistakably clear after the tightening of noose of the foreign debt trap in 1991. Still we are mad begging for inflow of foreign investments as if it is the only path of salvation for the country. This is strongly propagated by Indian bureaucracy and many scholars whose knowledge is very superficial and largely bookish. What is not realised that the drag on the process of industrialisation in India was not caused because of lack of funds rather it was the inadequate demand for industrial good which was the main hurdle. Bihar is no exception to this. Moreover, given the situational dynamics, both in India and abroad, there is no possibility of any significant inflow of foreign investment in the country.

But then all that the Indian and the state governments have been concerned all these years is how to increase receipts so that governments are able to increase their expenditures, particularly the plan expenditures. The proportion of plan expenditure which the non-understanding Indians accept as governmental effort for development, to total budgetary expenditure has not only been declining but has been almost insignificant in recent times. The recent five years period (Beginning from 1988-89) for which firm (i.e., actual) estimates are available, provide the following evidence.

Year	Percentage of Plan expenditure to total budgetary outlay of the Central and State Govt. ernment and Union Territories (Actuals)
1988-89	37.41
1989-90	35.18
1990-91	33.06
1991-92	32.48
1992-93	32.24

The annual growth of plan expenditure during this period has been 11.84 while the prices have been rising at an average rate of 10.65 per cent year. Thus, in real terms the annual growth of plan expenditure has been about one per cent. It is needless to emphasis that not only almost entire non-plan expenditure is spent on salaries and emoluments of employees but a significant proportion of the plan expenditure is diverted for the same end. Then, only a part of the plan expenditure is meant for poverty eradication and employment generation schemes for the poor. Here also, as per the assertion of the Indian Prime Minister, Rajiv Gandhi, in 1985, only 30 per cent of such funds reaches the poor. The states are even more poorly placed than the centre because they can not print currency notes nor they enjoy the unbridled power to raise loans and all the elastic and buoyant taxes are with the Centre and it also enjoys the power to ruthlessly curtail the mining royalties of the States. Moreover, the inflationary pressure generated by the centre is also a source of uncalled for liability for the states in terms of enhanced dearness allowances and other costs. Does not all these suggest that the entire edifice of governance in this country is costly and counter

Table-3

Percentage of Annual Average Rate of Growth

Period	Index of Agricultural Production	Index of Industrial Production 1980-81 Prices	Gross Domestic Product at	Rupee Value of US dollar	General Wholesale Price index	Employment in the orga. Sector
1951-52 to 1955-56	3.3	7.3	3.6	0.0 (-)	2.5	2.6
1986-87 to 1990-91	4.5	8.4	6.3	8.1	7.8	1.4
1991-92 to 1995-96	2.0	5.9	4.7*	14.0	10.0	0.8

Source: Government of India, *Economic Survey* for different years

* These are taken from the *Economic Survey* 1995 where these data for 1991-92 to 1993-94 got upward revised as compared to *Economic Survey* 1994.

Table-4

Percentage to Net National Product at Factor cost (NNP)

Period	Net Domestic Savings.	Net inflow of Investment 1980-81 Prices	Net domestic Capital formation	Foreign indebtedness (Year End)	Interest on Foreign Loans	Net out flow of factor income
1951-52 to 1955-56	6.2	0.4	6.6	1.5*	0.03	0.2
1986-87 to 1990-91	15.3	3.6	18.9	39.1**	0.8	1.4
1991-92 to 1995-96	16.3	1.1	17.4	42.1***	1.4	2.5

* Year-ending 1995-56 to NNP 1955-56

** Year-ending 1990-91 to NNP 1990-91

*** Year-ending 1995-96 to NNP 1995-96

Source: Government of India, *National Accounts Statistics and Economic Survey* for different years.

productive for growth of this economy? Or is that the entire government developmental effort has been directed towards keeping in comfort those who directly or indirectly draw emolument from the government and constitute only 6 per cent of the Indian workers? Will Bihar also go the same way?

It is a well established thesis that in the present technological syndrome, 'growth with social justice' requires some infrastructural support by the State. In Bihar which is essentially an agricultural economy and where its agricultural production depends on the vagaries of nature, the least that the State could do for rapid agricultural growth is to provide infrastructural support in terms of water management and electricity. It is needless to emphasise that rapid agricultural growth and concomitant enhanced income of rural Bihar (about 87 per cent of State's population) leading to escalated demand for industrial goods is the essential precondition for industrialisation of Bihar. It is also a well settled dictum that infrastructural support in absence of people's local initiative is mostly wasted and often has proved to be counter productive. Therefore, what is needed is not only local level autonomy in economic matters but infrastructural support related to water management and power sectors as well, which will require a level of decentralisation so as to enthuse local involvement. History has been witness to the fact that people's local experiences have been the main cause of the successes of large bulk of water management schemes and that local level maintenance and distribution in power sector have been responsible for avoidance of many ills which have been plaguing the giant power supply network in many Third World countries. The role of bureaucracy in economic matters has to be drastically minimised. Will Bihar make a break with the past?

References

1. Gandhi, M.K., *Harijan*, July 28, 1946, p. 236.
2. Jagmohan Singh and Chamanlal, (Edited 1987), *Bhagat Singh Aur Unke Sathion Ke Dastawaij* (Hindi), Revised Edition, Rajkamal Paperbaks. 1991, p. 86.
3. Lohia, Rammanohar (1963; Marx, *Gandhi and Socialism*, Second Edition 1978, pp. 135 and 380-81.
4. *Selected Works of Jawaharlal Nehru*, Orient Longman 1977, Vol. 14, p. 143.
5. Ibid., Vol. 10, p. 258, see also p. 125.
6. Gandhi, M.K., *Young India*. October 7, 1926, p. 348.
7. Lohia, Rammanohar, op. cit., p. 13.
8. Ibid., p. 16.
9. Selected Works of Jawaharlal Nehru, op. cit., Vol. 3, p. 378.

•

Infrastructure for Rural Development

S.K. Bose

The following constitute the infrastructure for any development:

1. Power, 2. Transport, 3. Market Organisation, 4. Credit, and 5. Storage.

The Rural Economy is basically agricultural, though rural industrialisation is, and has to be increasingly important. Whether it is agricultural or non-agricultural production, what ever is produced has to be progressively developed. Development of production means not only that the total output has to go up, but the output per head, has to go up, because the essence of development is that income per head has to increase.

In a market economy, any produce has to reach the market, and for that it is necessary that transport should be available to carry the produce.

After the agricultural produce is harvested, the farmer should have a place where he can temporarily keep his produce. But many farmers do not have that facility.

After the produce is harvested, therefore the traders come and purchase the crops against advances given earlier. The farmer is forced to accept the advance much before the crop is harvested always in need of money. Therefore the bulk of the produce that because of the limitations stated above, as also because he is reaches the organised market is actually brought by the traders, rather than the farmer. The difference between the harvest price and the price which the consumer pays is therefore pocketed by the trader.

Even from before the transfer of power, or even before the 2nd War, some steps were taken to organise agricultural markets. After the transfer of power a lot more has been done. The regulated market, popularly known as Bazaar Samities were purported to be an answer to this need of the farmer to get a correct price for his produce.

The functioning of the Bazaar Samiti has been handicapped by the absence of good roads. The Bazaar Samiti, under the administrative control of the State level Marketing Board, are known to be earning profits. One of the approved purposes to which the profits of the agricultural Marketing Boards may be utilised is building of roads. These roads should be built not only within the Market Yard but gradually cover the hinterland. Little progress has been made in this regard so far.

Excepting the Bazaar Samiti situated in Urban Centres. Such samities in Rural areas, few as they are, are not known to have contributed much to building of roads connecting their Yards to the hinterland.

Most States have a rural Engineering Department. The prime responsibility for building the rural roads rests on this Department but they are handicapped for want of resources.

Construction and maintenance of the National Highways is a responsibility of the Central Government but as a matter of convenience, maintenance of National Highway within a State is actually done by the State Government though the funds for the same are made available by the central Government only new roads that may be built in any part of the country are the responsibility of the central P. W.D. It is an unfortunate fact that National Highways whose maintenance cost are borne by the Central Government are not properly maintained by the state Government concerned, with of course some exceptions.

By and large roads in the Eastern region, including Bihar and West Bengal, are in a poor state of maintenance.

It is easy to understand that the key to economic re-generation is trade, and that trade depends upon Transport. Railway even now carry the bulk of the commodities that are traded but so far as supplies up to and from the Railway stations are concerned roads have to be there. It is this aspect of the problem which is known as Rail-Road Co-ordination.

Market Organisation

The preceding paragraphs have referred to the need for an adequate market organisation so that the farmer can get a good price for his produce.

Even before the IInd War, efforts were made by the cooperative movement to form Marketing cooperatives. These became fairly important in respect of those crops which constituted raw materials for industry. Sugarcane Co-operatives in Bihar and Uttar Pradesh became fairly important. They were followed by Maharashtra which now is the largest grower of sugarcane and the largest manufacturer of cane sugar. In Maharaastra the cane sugar Co-operative have became so important that some of them have even opened the Sugar Factories.

These farmers Co-operatives and the sugar Industry have not only provided a good example of upward vertical integration, but down ward integration also in the form of starting fertilizers factories, e.g. the fertilizer factories started by the IFFCO.

Unfortunately the Cane Co-operatives in Bihar and to some extent in U.P. have not proved to be equally successful. Attempts to organise Jute growers into marketing Co-operativies have however not achieved similar success. In Maharashtra Cotton growers have not only formed Marketing Co-operativies but have demonstrated a similar tendency of upward vertical integration in respect of ginning and baling the raw cotton, thereby enabling every farmer to extend their control to the initial stages of the processing of raw cotton.

To the extent that the Co-operativies of farmers can organise themselves successfully, they can get a better price for their produce and also take a share of the profits of the processing of agricultural produce.

The well known name AMUL is a supreme example of how milk producers have achieved vertical upward integration and captured a major part of the market for not only liquid milk but also milk products.

It is sad that Bihar has not been able to show a similar progress in respect of Marketing Co-operativies except in recent years because of the interest taken by the All India Dairy Development Board.

Storage

An essential part of marketing is storage. The picture that was drawn up by the advocates of Co-operation included godowns under the control of Marketing Unions. In Bihar the BISCOMAUN is an example of an apex body for marketing of agricultural produce. Unfortunately the BISCOMAUN has become more of a distribution agency for fertilizer in short supply rather than an organisation for assisting agricultural produces to get a better price for their produce. The majority of the Agricultural Marketing Boards are content with building Marketing Yards in some selected places and making a profit for themselves by charging a fee, without going lower down to be able to reach the actual farmers and deal with them directly. The middle men have not been eliminated.

The Rural Credit Survey Committee appointed by the Researve Bank of India in 1951 and reporting in 1954 death with the need for organising marketing and linking it with credit and storage, and had presented an outline of an organisation for the farmers which, if properly implemented could have brought about a real change in the picture of rural life.

Credit

The most important recommendation of the Rural Credit Survey Committee was for nationalising the Imperial Bank of India and re-naming it as the State Banks of India. The State Bank of India came into being on the 1st of July, 1955 and has grown into not only the biggest Bank in the country, but as one of the biggest Banks in the World, on account of the number of branches, the size of deposits and the number of accounts of customers.

The reason behind the Rural Survey Committee's recommendation for Nationalizing the Imperial Bank was large number of branches that it possessed, making it easy to transfer funds from one part of the country to another.

The Rural Banking Enquiry Committee which preceded it pointed out the difficulty in respect of transfer of funds, but had not made any specific suggestion of the nature that the Rural Co-operative Survey Committee had made except in respect of remittance of funds.

The Survey Committee emphasised the need to release the farmers from the clutches of the money lender-cum-trader-cum Landlord. When the Survey Committee made its report Land lordism was not abolished. Therefore the Survey Committee had spoken of the money lender-cum-trader-cum-landlord complex representing the combined trinity, like the mythological Brahma, Vishnu and Maheshwara.

The Re-organisation of Rural Credit which the Survey Committee recommended, unfortunately, proceeded from the top, with the establishment of special funds in the Reserve Bank of India for reorganising the Rural Credit Structure.

Subsequently these special funds got merged with a new Institution, namely the National Agricultural Bank for Reconstruction and Development (NABARD). This organisation is now the apex national body for dealing with agricultural credit.

A new type of Banks namely Regional Rural Banks have been set up a few year ago, which also are connected with the NABARD.

There is demand, recently voiced by the officers and employees of Regional Rural Banks that a separate national apex body for Regional Rural Banks be set-up.

The country had from before the 2nd War the Land Mortgage Banks which are supposed to land for long terms.

The land mortgage Banks aas also the state Co-operative Banks are all connected with the NABARD. Therefore there is a feeling that the hands of the NABARD are too full. Hence the demand for a national apex body for Regional Rural Banks.

Besides these special institutions we have the traditional Commercial Banks which have over the last 20 years opened a large number of rural branches.

We have therefore a multiplicity of credit Institutions, which is a little confusing. What is needed is not the opening of a new Institution, but their strengthening. The one malady that is common to all the financial Institutions working in Rural areas is non-realisation of advances which are now emphemestically described as non-performing assets.

To top it all, there are political gimmics indulged in by politicians. When loans upto a certain limit, normally Rs. 10,000/- are remitted by the Government. It is learnt that the financial burden of this remission falls not on the Government but on the financial institutions, which thereby earn a bad name, resulting in the eating up of their capital. Unless this situation is remedied, mere structural reform will not be of any help.

It is said that non-payment of dues is a malady afflicting more the bigger farmers who are socially and politically influential. The Regional Rural Banks as also the Co-operative Credit Societies should restrict their activities to only the small and marginal farmers. As was suggested by the Rural Credit Survey Committee the bulk of agricultural loans according to the Survey Committee Report was to be given by the Co-operative societies and the Commercial Banks should be in the field for crop loans Methods were devised whereby the loan is to be given not in cash, but in kind, i.e. seeds, fertilizers etc. Theoretically this system should not have failed, except for the bureaucratic red tape and corruption. It is now an open secret that loans neither from co-operative Credit Societies, Regional Rural Bank branches or Commercial Banks can be available at their face value, without deduction at the source even while the loan is being paid.

Similar corruption is stated to be associated with intermediate period loans, for purchase of draft animal or even loans for milch cattle.

Therefore the problem is how to make the credit machinery more efficient and free from corruption.

Marketing and Price

The essence of development is increase in rural incomes. Improvement in income is dependent not only on increase in output but also on the price which the output will fetch in the market.

As mentioned earlier, the essence of the cultivator deprivation of a proper share of the market price is his inability to hold stocks. Attempts at improving storage facilities for rural produce, particularly agricultural produce is sought to be remedied by warehousing facilities. A pre tier structure of warehouses has been built up after the submission of the report of the Rural Credit Survey Committee. How far this structure is functioning in another question.

Prices

As mentioned earlier the aim of marketing re-organisation is to enable the produce to get a proper care of the market price. Apart from storage associated with credit, these days market prices are considerably influence by Government after harvest and procurement is affected at the prices announced. The government has to maintain a balance between the interest of consumer and those of the producer.

In view of the importance of the rural vote Bank, over the last several years procurement prices are going up steadily. The question is how much of these higher prices goes to the grower. By and large the general impression is that it is the big grower who can manage to get a proper share of the market price. The output of small grower which is concerned by the middle man, does not bring proper income to him. The essence of re-organisation of the marketing structure together with the storage and warehousing facilities is to give small grower the advantage of high market prices. The Co-operative Marketing Structure has failed to meet to this goal.

The Social Infrastructure for Rural Development

A sum of Rs. 36 thousand crores is to be spent during the 8th Five Year Plan on Rural Development. What will be the agencies through which this money will be spent? Recent discussion, including the statement of the Prime Minister indicates that the Gram Panchayats will be the principal agency for implementing the Rural Development Programme.

The 8th Five Year Plan will be over in another two years. A number of States, including Bihar has not yet held Elections to Gram Panchayat. The Prime Minister had stated that those States which will not complete Elections to the Gram Panchayat will be deprived of the grants for the Rural Development under the 8th Plan. This will be a punishment more for the people than for the State Government.

There is no doubt that a democratically constituted and decentralised agency like the Gram Panchayet would theoretically be the best guarantee against misuse of funds for development.

The basic question is how effective will the elected members of the Gram Panchayat be? The Gram Sabha is the soverign body for Gram Panchayat. This means the entire adult village population. How effective will this village adult population be?

We have been having adult suffrage from 1952. We claim to be the largest democracy in the world in terms of population. But does power today really rest with the people?

Infrastructure for Rural Development

Shree Shankar Sharan

A great deal of money is allocated for rural development every year but it seldom seems to be self sustaining. It gets spent on JRY or IRDP or Employment guarantee schemes. While public spending to generate more employment and incomes to ward off destitution or starvation is laudable, its capacity to sustain itself depends on the extent to which it adds to the rural infrastructure and thereby to productivity of land, still the mainstay of rural life.

The kind of infrastructure needed is sources of irrigation, power, roads, drainage and credit and at the level of human capital education and health. I should like to start with credit, the life line of rural development, since savings and capital formation in villages is small and credit is a crying need for everything from asset creation to consumption. The Central Government have created some excellent institutions e.g. NABARD to provide low interest finance to cooperatives to lend to farmers to improve or create rural assets. Cooperatives in the entire country have flourished with such credit. The sugarcane cooperative in Maharashtra is a shining example, some of them have set up their own sugar mills. Tragically in Bihar our cooperatives were captured by a mafia which has killed the movement and very often misappropriated funds. Fictitions loans or budget loans were granted to farmers beyond loans actually received by them and beyond their repaying ability. The cooperative movement in Bihar has almost died. However, good men have succeeded in reviving flourishing milk operatives in North Bihar. The movement has still a lot of potential left in Bihar but needs reorganization. I suggest that Gram Panchayats should themselves constitute local cooperation grant loans and recover them. Bad law and order vandalism and poor repaying habit have discouraged Bank loans in rural areas. I suggest that Bank credit should also be extended through Panchayats to make repayments easier.

The power situation in most parts of the country and all parts of Bihar is precarious. Thanks to private and farms enterprise, a net-work of tubewells has sprung up in Bihar specially North Bihar, in which water table is high but they generally use diesel pumps because electricity is scarce or non existent or prohibitively expensive because of malpractices in electricity Boards. If power were plentiful and cheap the network could grow further. Malpractices in the Board also add to the farmers woes and a deterrent to using electricity. I have known farmers who have switched over from electricity to diesel because of harassment by the Revenue offices of the Electricity Board. A massive expansion of power generation and distribution by inducting private investment is needed. The example of Dabhol must be a deterrent to foreign investment in our power sector. Our politicians must learn to keep power and politics apart. Private management of power must also be encouraged because of the rampant and incurable corruption in Electricity Boards. Most of the Boards deserve to be scrapped and their staff disbanded for making things worse rather than better in the power sector. The good ones among them can find jobs in the private sector. It gives me no pleasure to make this drastic recommendation, but drastic situation require drastic remedies.

The next requirement is of roads. A very large number of villages in Bihar are still unconnected by road and whatever roads exist are in shambles. We are able to reach Bathanitola, the site of a recent massacre, only by walking 6 kms from the nearest canal road. It was the case with Belchi also, another site of massacre. The grim law and order situation is partly due to a poor road network carrying fertilizer or food products or building material or machines e.g. pumping set to or from many villages, is too time taking expensive and arduous. If lampens rural development, Devolution of power and funds to Gram Panchayats and Zila Parishads alone is capable of remedying the situation. The maintenance of roads should also be made the responsibility of local Government invested with requisite power and funds. Perhaps we should resort to a labour tax for the poor instead of tax in cash to encourage voluntary and free labour on roads and canals.

Yet another requirement is of canals, water courses and drainages. Because of increasing unrest against large dams and large irrigation works, we should plan for small dams and small irrigation projects including water conservation schemes and check dams in rural areas.

In the larger rivers construction of large dams could be fruitful but their cost will be heavy and opposition to them sincere from the environmental angle. We should perhaps be content with building large pumping stations to pump water from major rivers into new water channels. We have been wasting precious water by not creating these channels from the Ganga, Sone and other large rivers if the Jamuna could colate Rajasthan, surely Ganga and Sone water could be made to irrigate the drought prone districts of Gaya, Palamu, Rothas, Jamui, Santhal Pargana, Hazaribagh etc. If this cannot work, a few more barrages on major rivers may be necessary.

A more important task is the maintenance of our irrigation works which are failing apart like the Sone canal. Work on them should be taken up by Government but Gram Panchayats also involved in their maintenance. Perhaps it is here that we could initiate a labour tax in lieu of irrigation rate in cash.

The Irrigation Department seems to require greater motivation to work. The Department, I suggest should be placed under the Chief Minister with an eminent engineer as his minister of state. A Joint Committee of the Central and State Government should oversee the construction and maintenance of major irrigation work. A portion should be set a part in the panchayat funds for undertaking and maintaining minor irrigation. The Panchayats should also be charged with the responsibility of building field channel which take many years in Bihar to complete.

The education and health fronts have virtually collapsed in Bihar and on the road to collapse in the rest of India. We are caught in a vicious circle. Being poor or powerful makes us greedy as teachers and doctors and greed adds to our poverty and misery. Neglect of teaching and the unbridled ambitions of the powerful add to student discontent indiscipline and resort to unfair practices. Similarly medical neglect has multiplied our health problem several fold and gravely put at risk the lives and health of our people in our outlying areas. The collapse of education threaten both our children and the nation with grave consequences.

We are passing through social ferment. Those who abuse their power will one day have to pay for it. It is not past our wisdom to correct the problem of setback in education and health. Power to zila parishads, Gram panchayts will largely correct it. Even now things will improve if chronic misbehaviour is treated drastically by wholesale dismissal. We hope our powerful CM will heed this advice.

Both sectors are funds starved. Private institutions should be encouraged in both sectors, will education commercialised with concessional seats reserved for poor students. Good teachers and doctors should be handsomely rewarded and honoured.

The Central Government have lately offered concession for investments in rural infrastructure. We should make haste to avail them.

Lastly the prerequisite of all development is an environment of security, peace and rule of law, which is sadly declining. Before investment takes care of infrastructure, the state and the political parties should have an agreed programme not to mix development with divisive politics and not hammer its smooth progress. Since infrastructure will create jobs it will also contribute to improving the security, besides the economic environment.

•

Recommendations of the Workshop

Recommendations of the workshop "Challenges in Rural Development" organised by Lal Bahadur Shashtri Institute of Rural Management and Rural Development, Patna, from 28th October to 30th October, 1994.

I. General

Despite the various efforts made in the sphere of Rural Development no substantial improvement has been made in the levels of living in the Rural areas. This requires a rethinking on the entire issue of rural development.

II. Selecting schemes for Rural Development

Different schemes of rural development envisage devolution of huge funds in rural areas for generating employment with an end to ameliorate rural poverty. This approach leads to a thrust from above in areas of under-development without making any effort to assess the local resources and local needs and aspirations of the beneficiaries. This creates a situation in which every programme is considered as a programme of the government resulting in apathy of the local people in its implementation. This process leads to near stagnation of the situation of non-development where people's participation is missing. This adverse situation can be changed if areas specific programmes are formulated taking into account the existing local resources and requirements. This calls for empowerment of Gram Sabhas which could formulate their individual programmes. Integration of all such programmes should form the district plan which should lead to compilation of various areas specific programmes for rural development in a particular state. Government of India, therefore, should devise a system wherein funds are released to particular state after considering its programme requirements. It is good that Government of India have been sending money directly to the DRDA, but the DRDA should be streamlined to have full knowledge of the requirements of the panchayats and specific areas of development. This approach should equally address itself for improving the human capital of the area largely through investment in education controlled population and improving communicational facilities.

III. Infrastructure Requirement for Rural Development

(i) Arrangements for training of individuals and agencies associated with rural development including government functionaries should be made at the state, district, block and Panchayat levels so as to acquaint them with the latest development in the field of rural development and motivate them for effective performance to accelerate the pace of development.

(ii) The administrative machinery should be so inter-woven that there is a perfect coordination between panchayat level functioning and state level planning. This coordination can be achieved at block and village levels through common training, periodic meetings and appropriate monitoring.

(iii) There should be effective and functional coordination between the Block level consultative committee and the Block level Banker's Committee for adequate functioning of the Rural Credit Agencies and smooth flow of credit.

(iv) Infrastructure facilities both quantitatively and qualitatively need to be improved; rural roads, irrigation facilities, rural electrification should be given due importance in any programme of rural development.

(v) The Panchayat Beneficiaries Sub Committee, Area Beneficiaries Advisory Committee and Block Level Beneficiaries Advisory Committee should be constituted and made functional in each Panchayat and Block.

(vi) The time taken in decision making proves at the district, block and village levels in identification, sanctions and implementation of the scheme should be minimised.

(vii) The remote and inaccessible areas under the influence of Naxalite and extremists should be given top priority in development works.

IV. Panchayat Raj

(a) Under the recent constitutional amendments, the Gram Panchayats have been empowered to undertake and execute all schemes of rural development. This will however be really effective if the beneficiaries are organised into functional groups so that they try themselves to manage the schemes properly without any reliance on outside agencies.

(b) Within the ambit of the existing provisions of the Panchayati Raj Act, the induction of persons below the poverty line should be ensured not only for safeguarding their interest but activising their involvement in over all developmental activities of the panchayats.

(c) The size of the Panchayat as currently envisaged in the Bihar Act should be reduced both in the plains and hill areas to make it more viable for exploiting available resources for its integrated development.

V. Participation and Motivation

(i) Participation and involvement of the people in the identification, preparation and implementation of the schemes meant for their development are very important.

(ii) The task of socio-economic uplift requires persons having desire and will to bring about the desirable change through devotion in motivating people towards the target.

VI. Unemployment and Poverty

Eradication of unemployment will automatically lead to alleviation of poverty and unless the former is achieved the attempt to accomplish the latter will be like running after a mirage.

VII. Identification of Beneficiaries in Poverty Alleviation Programme

(a) Identification of the prospective beneficiaries of all poverty alleviation schemes should be done afresh with the involvement of such people themselves. Such list should be updated every three years.

(b) Similarly identification of districts for purposes of special programmes like EAS and RPDS (Employment Assurance Scheme and Revamped Public Distribution System) should be done afresh having regard to the poverty ratio, and per capita income in the district.

VIII. Population and Rural Development

Containment of Population Growth is an important part of the Rural Development Programme and hence such rural families which practice family planning norms should get governmental benefits on priority basis.

IX. Rural Credit

1. The rural credit delivery system particularly in the State of Bihar requires to be reorganised and strengthened so as to ensure regular flow of institutional credit for agriculture and rural development. This requires the following:

(i) Writing off loans or postponement of recovery on political and populist considerations should be stopped.

(ii) Delayed, untimely and sometimes inadequate dispensation of IRDP loans should be avoided so as to arrest the large scale misutilisation and default of credit.

(iii) Loans to beneficiaries under IRDP and other agricultural and development programmes should be advanced on the identification by the Banks and financing Institutions directly. The system of recommendatory or directed lending should be discontinued.

(iv) The heavy incident of overdues particularly in Bihar State has eroded the credit absorbing capacity not only of the individual borrowers but also of the lending Institutions and requires to be tackled on an urgent basis. The active co-operation and assistance of the State Government functionaries particularly in regard to recovery of wilfull defaults must be available to the Co-operative Banks, RRBs and Commercial Banks, functioning in the State.

2. The rural rich apart from buying tractors, sinking the tubewells and using fertilisers and improved seeds, do not invest enough in agriculture. They have not diversified either in the pattern of cropping, growing cash crops or in the agro-industries sector. The last is the big virgin field open for the enterprising farmer. He needs support in terms of information, willing and ready finance, helpful and unexploitative or banking structure and marketing facilities.

X. Land Reforms

(i) Effective implementation of land reforms covering ownership rights, enforcement of land ceiling, distribution of surplus lands and updating of land records is a must to augment usefulness of the rural development programmes.

(ii) Also forcible occupation of land and illegal cutting of harvest have depleted the cultivation and has positively harmed agricultural output as well as the interest of agricultural labourers who are forced to migrate elsewhere in search of livelihood.

(iii) Rule of law must prevail in agrarian dispute, violence harms the interest of those for whom it is perpetuated.

(iv) The subdivision and fragmentation of land under the succession laws must stop. The law should be amended to provide that land cannot be subdivided below 5 acres and must be held and farmed jointly.

XI. Non-Conventional Source of Energy and Rural Development

(a) Lack of power is turning farmers to the more expensive diesal causing increase in cost of inputs. Therefore regular supply of electricity to farmers would decrease the cost of agricultural production and also help in increased production.

(b) Non-conventional energy, specially solar energy and renewable e.g., Gobar gas energy should be tried out for cottage industry. We should learn to be self-dependent in power.

XII. Women and Rural Development

(i) The rural women should be organised to undertake and participate in the implementation of socio economic developmental activities of their areas for which self help groups may be constituted and proper institutional finance should be made available.

(ii) Unmarried, separated and individual woman should be associated as beneficiaries under IRDP, TRYSEM and DWCRA.

XIII. Agro- based Industry

Areas specific programmes for development of agro based rural and cottage industries should be promoted on an extensive scale by preparing and implementing comprehensive plan of rural industrialiation based on available skill, inputs etc.

XIV. Education and Rural Development

Education opens the door for development. An all out effort should be made for the uinversalization of elementary education through both formal and non-formal streams. Weaker sections of the people including women can be empowered through this route. It would also enable them to fight injustice and exploitation and promote both social and psychic mobility.

XV. Rural Health Programme

For sound and effective Rural Health programme, the existing system of recruitment, transfer and posting of medical officers should be decentralised to Zonal agencies which should have doctors committed for the health development programmes of that particular zone. Because commitment to community is a must and takes a life time to achieve it.

XVI. Role of NGOs

(a) The activists and the NGOs working in the field of rural development should create awareness among the aforesaid segment of the population through training programmes. Group discussions and regular contacts so as to prepare them to come forward and participate in the Election process for running the Panchayats.

(b) The poor are reluctant to participate in developmental activities partly due to barrier of caste, religion, social forces and presence of affluent influential groups and largely due to lack of appropriate and adequate transmission of information, NGOs and self help group can ameliorate this situation.

(c) To accelarate the pace of rural development voluntary agencies should be encouraged to take up innovative tasks. Some of these projects may be financed through the government. To achieve results in this direction voluntary agencies with dedication and good record should be chosen.

XVI. Role of Media

Both print and electronic media should acquaint the rural masses about development programmes taken up by the government and voluntary agencies and motivate them for participating enthusiastically in the execution of these programmes.

•

List of Participants

1.	Anil Sinha	Secretary, Rajbhasha Dept. Government of Bihar, Patna.
2.	Amrendra	Research Officer, A.N. S. Institute of Social Studies, Patna.
3.	Arun Prasad	Former Chairman, Bihar State Subordinate Service Comm., Rukunpura, Bailey Road, Patna.
4.	A.K. Rath	Addl. Industrial Dev. Commissioner, Government of Bihar, Vikas Bhawan, Patna.
5.	A.K. Jha	Reader in Pol. Sc., A.N. Sinha Institute of Social Studies, Patna.
6.	Arif Hassan	Reader in Social Psychology A.N. Sinha Institute of Social Studies, Patna.
7.	Arbind Kr. Choudhary	Asstt. Prof. Dept. of Agril. Econ. RAU, Pusa, Samastipur, Bihar.
8.	Ashok Kr. Sinha	Secretary Mahila Shiksha Vikas Sansthan, Vill: Ramnagar Math Par, P.O.: Bansbigha, Dhanarua, Patna 804451.
9.	Atamanand	Professor, Economics Division, L.N. Mishra Institute, Patna.
10.	Dr. B.D. Prasad	Social Activist and eminent orthopedic Surgeon (FRCS), Langar Toli, Patna.
11.	B.P. Gupta	President, Bihar Industry Association
12.	Bhagwan Pd. Singh	Reader, Department of Economics, Patna University, Patna.
13.	B.P. Gupta	Free Lancer, Journalist, New Karbighahia, Patna , 800 020.

14.	B.B. Mandal	Reader in Sociology, A.N. Sinha Institute of Social Stud ies, Patna.
15.	Daisey Narain	Professor, Deptt. of History, Patna Women's College, P.U.
16.	D.D. Guru	Professor of Economics, A.N. Sinha Institute of Social Studies, Patna.
17.	D.C. Murmu	Representative of TISCO, Tata Steel Rural Dev. Society of Janandolan, Dhanbad.
18.	D. Sahay	Research Officer, A.N. Sinha Institute of Social Studies, Patna.
19.	G.N. Tiwari	President, VIVEK, Rajendra Nagar, Road No. 2, Patna-16.
20.	H.K. Sahay	Prof. and Head of the Department of Economics, Patna University, Patna.
21.	H.R. Mishra	Former Vice Chancellor, Birsa Agriculture University (Ranchi).
22.	H.K. Sinha	Former Addl. Secretary, Deptt. of HRD and Executive Director Lal Bahadur Shastri Institute of Rural Management and Rural Development, Patna.
23.	H.B. Lal	Former Chief Engineer (Rural Electrification) Bihar State Electricity Board.
24.	I.C. Kumar	Administrator, BISCOMAUN, Patna and Former Commissioner cum Secretary Food and Civil Sup plies Dept. Government of Bihar.
25.	Indradeo Sharma	Reader in Economics, A.N. Sinha Institute of Social Studies, Patna.
26.	Indu Bharati	Research Officer, A.N. Sinha Institute of Social Studies, Patna.
27.	Jyotindra Mohan Prasad	Former Director General of Police, Bansi Kunj, Patna.
28.	J.N. Tiwari	Professor of Economics, Patna University, Patna.

29.	J.K.P.Verma	Former Addl. Distt. Magistrate, Patna, B-1/2, Godavari Apartment, Ashiana Road, Raja Bazar, Patna.
30.	J.P. Srivastav	Former Secretary, BISCOMAU.
31.	K.K. Srivastava	Former Chief Secretary, Bihar, 31-A, Srikrishnapuri, Patna.
32.	K.P. Sinha	Former Commissioner and Secretary to Government of Bihar, North Srikrishnapuri, Patna.
33.	K.C. Saha	Secretary, Dept. of Higher Education, Government of Bihar and Director, A.N. Sinha Institute of Social Studies, Patna.
34.	Kamalesh Kumar	University Professor of Extension Education, Haryana Agricultural University, Hisar.
35.	K.K. Verma	Professor of Sociology and Anthropology, A.N. Sinha Institute of Social Studies, Patna.
36.	K.K. Vidyarathy	Advocate and Social Activist, 124, Pataliputra Colony, Patna
37.	K. Amrendra	Representative of Syndicate Bank, Patna.
38.	L. Dayal	Former Chief Secretary, Bihar, 177, P.P. Colony, Patna-13.
39.	K. Mohan	Sadhnapuri, Patna.
40.	M.K. Aggraval	Chief General Manager, State Bank of India, Bihar, Patna.
41.	M. Mohiuddin	Former Chairman, Bihar Public Service Commission and Former Vice Chancellor, Patna University, Patna. 7 Dinkar Path, Patna, Rajendra Nagar.
42.	M.N. Karna	Former Director, A.N. Sinha Institute of Social Studies, Patna. Professor of Sociology, N.E. Hill University, Shillong.
43.	Maya Sharan	Principal, Shambhu Sharan Mahila College, Kadam Kuan, Patna.

44.	Meera Verma	Professor of Economics, Magadh Mahila College, Patna.
45.	Meera Datta	Member All India High Court Employees Federation, Patna.
46.	M.M. P. Srivastava	Formerly Additional Director Agriculture Bihar, Representing Sulabh International. Patna.
47.	Manohar Lal	Reader in Sociology, A.N. Sinha Institute of Social Studies, Patna.
48.	Mahesh Chandra Jha	Secretary, Manav Samridhi Sansthan M/ 314, S.K. Puri, Patna.
49.	M.L. Jha	Coordinator, Centre for R.D. and Management, Bihar Vidyapeeth, Patna-10.
50.	M. Akram Ali	Patna.
51.	M.P. Sinha	4, West Anandpuri, Patna
52.	Dr. Narendra Prasad	FRCS and Eminent Surgeon, Doctor's Colony, Kankarbagh, Patna.
53.	Nil Ratan	Reader in Pol. Sc., A. N. Sinha Institute of Social Studies, Patna.
54.	Neeraj Sharma	National Bank of Rural Development, Maurya Lok, Patna.
55.	Pradhan H. Prasad	Professor Emeritus, Former Director A.N. Sinha Institute of Social Studies, Patna.
56.	Prabhakar Kr.	Kiran Niwas, South Mandiri, Patna.
57.	P.P. Ghosh	Reader in Statistics, A.N.S. Institute of Social Studies, Patna.
58.	P. Pancham	Representative of Press Trust of India
59.	Priyadarshi	Janashakti Sangharsh Vahini, Sri Krishna Nagar, Patna.
60.	Ranchor Pd.	Former Dy. Chairman, Bihar State Planning Board, 145, Pataliputra Colony, Patna.

61.	Raji Ahmad	Director, Gandhi Sangrahalaya, Patna.
62.	Ramola Nandi	Former Director Higher Education, Government of Bihar, Former Principal, Magadh Mahila Collelge, Patna. The Shyamashru, off Mazharul Haq Path, Patna.
63.	R.K. P.N. Singh	President, Industrial Estate, Patiliputra. Patna.
64.	R.P. Singh	Former Dean of Education. P.U. and Former Principal. Patna Training College and Emeritus Professor, Patna University, Patna.
65.	R. Prasad	Former Asstt. General Manager, TELCO. Kadamkuan, Patna.
66.	R. Dayal	Representative of the Times of India, Patna.
67.	Ram Nath Rajesh	Representative, Sandhya Prahari, Patna.
68.	R.P. Shah	Representative of Blitz, Bombay in Patna.
69.	R.N. Jha	Research Officer, A.N. Sinha Institute of Social Studies, Patna.
70.	R.K. Pandey	Research Officer, A.N. Sinha Institute of Social Studies, Patna.
71.	Radhakrishna	Representative, Nav Bharat Times, Patna
72.	Ram Nagina Singh	Advocate and Social Activist, Congress Maidan, Kadam Kaun, Patna.
73.	Raj Lakshmi Rath	Fellow, A.N. Sinha Institute of Social Studies, Patna.
74.	Rabindra Kishore	Research Officer, A.N. Sinha Institute of Social Studies, Patna.
75.	S.K. Bose	Chairman Bihar School Examination Board, Patna and Former Professor of Economics, Patna University, Patna.
76.	Lt. Gen. (Retd.) S.K. Sinha	Boring Canal Road, Patna

77.	Sachchidananda	Professor Emeritus, and Former Director, A.N. Sinha Institute of Social Studies, Patna.
78.	Shree Shankar Sharan	Former Development Commissioner, Bihar, Kadam Kuan, Patna.
79.	S.K. Sinha	Former Manager, Reserve Bank of India, D-5, Sadhnapuri, Patna.
80.	Sunil Sharan	Former Vice Chancellor, Bhagalpur University, Srinivas, Janak Kishore Road, Kadam Kuan, Patna.
81.	Shashi Shekhar	Association for Study and Action, 78, Birchand Patel Marg, Patna.
82.	S.N. Puri	Former Dy. Inspector General of Police, Pirmohani, Patna.
83.	Surya Narayan	Bapu Smarak Mahila Charakha Sangh, Kadam Kuan, Patna.
84.	S.K. Singh	Associate Professor, National Institute of Rural Development, Rajendranagar, Hyderabad (Representative of NIRD).
85.	Surendra Pd.	Representative of Researve Bank of India. Patna.
86.	Sunil Kumar	Research Officer, A.N. Sinha Institute of Social Studies, Patna.
87.	Sanjay Singh	Staff Reporter, The Hindustan Times, Patna.
88.	S. Narayan	Reader of Sociology and Anthropology, A.N. Sinha Institute of Social Studies, Patna.
89.	Shabeda Warsi	Sultanganj, Patna.
90.	Shivnath	Research Officer, A.N.. Sinha Institute of Social Studies, Patna.
91.	Shukla Mohanthy	Principal, Womens College, Chaibasa.
92.	Sunirmal Das	A.N. Sinha Institute of Social Studies, Patna.
93.	Tara Kishore Prasad	Senior Advocate, Kadam Kuan, Patna.

94.	Vinay Kr. Kanth	Director Asian Development Research, Instt. and Professor, B.N. College, Patna University, Patna.
95.	Vijya Kumar	Sampurna Kranti Vahini, Kadam Kuan, Patna.
96.	Virendra Mishra	Representative of Hindustan Dainik, Daily
97.	Vinod Kr. Ranjan	Mahendru, Patna.
98.	Y.L. Das	Senior Research Officer, A.N. S. Institute of Social Studies, Patna.

•